DEAR ARTIST

LAST LOOKS
PRESS

**LAST LOOKS
P R E S S**

Author Photo: Michael Roud
Publishing and Design Services: MelindaMartin.me

ISBN: 978-1-7360755-0-0 (paperback), 978-1-7360755-1-7 (epub)

matt christian

DEAR ARTIST

75 LETTERS FROM ONE STRUGGLING ARTIST TO ANOTHER

LAST LOOKS
PRESS

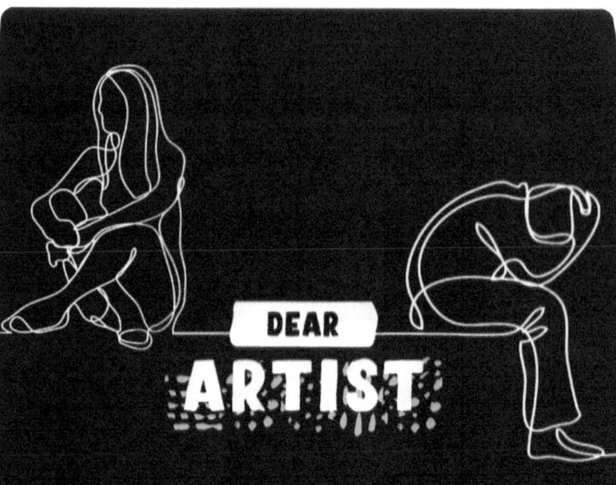
DEAR
ARTIST
THE
STRUGGLE
IS REAL.

INTRODUCTION

If you're holding this book, it was written for you.

I am an actor first and foremost. The stage and screen are my great loves. Every little aspect of performing and technique I could talk about with you for hours. I also dabble in writing, painting, and music. Having not had the proverbial "big break" yet, I know first hand what it's like slogging through the artistic trenches for years. I'm well acquainted with the muck, mire, desperation, and devastation that is found down there. In fact, it is there that most of these pages were born.

I wrote these letters as reminders to myself.

Whenever I found myself in a tough spot, or on the brink of giving up, one of these letters would often quietly emerge from my soul, reminding me to keep going, or to be patient, or to savor the beauty, or to ignore the people telling me it was time to call it quits.

This book isn't meant to be a "how-to" for creativity. It isn't meant as a guide for breaking into the industry of your choice. And while there might be bits and pieces of advice along the way, for the most part, it is simply meant to be what you need it to be in this moment of your journey.

Wherever you happen to find yourself.

Especially if you happen to be struggling.

Whether you're just starting out or already established in your creative field, none of us is immune to darkness.

My hope is that within these pages you find a shoulder to cry on, an ear who understands, and a reassurance that you aren't crazy. That you can do this. That this is the most sane thing you can be doing. And that you might take away a new perspective on the world and your unique artistic place in it.

We need your voice in this world. You can't give up. Not now. Not yet.

It's a struggle being an artist. Most of the time our paths can feel a lot less like following a dream and more like fighting a war. But no matter what, we're in this together. You, me and every other person in this world who holds the sacred title of Artist.

I don't have all the answers, and will never claim to. What I do have is a little bit of experience, a lot of ground traveled and hopefully an encouraging word along the way.

I hope this volume encourages, inspires, and motivates you to dig even deeper into your craft. To keep you from giving up just a little bit longer. And to remind you that, as much as it might feel like it, you are not alone.

May this book soothe your soul and give you something to cling to. You've been broken so many times. Let's see if we can't do some healing together.

DEAR ARTIST,

If there's something you've always wanted to do,
you owe it to your soul to try.
Better to look a fool today
than wake up with regrets at 90.

Pick up that guitar.
Those shoes won't dance themselves.
Your song might be the one to change the world.

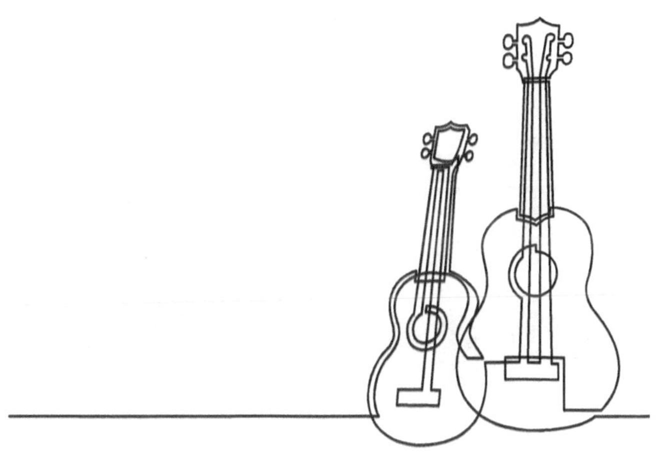

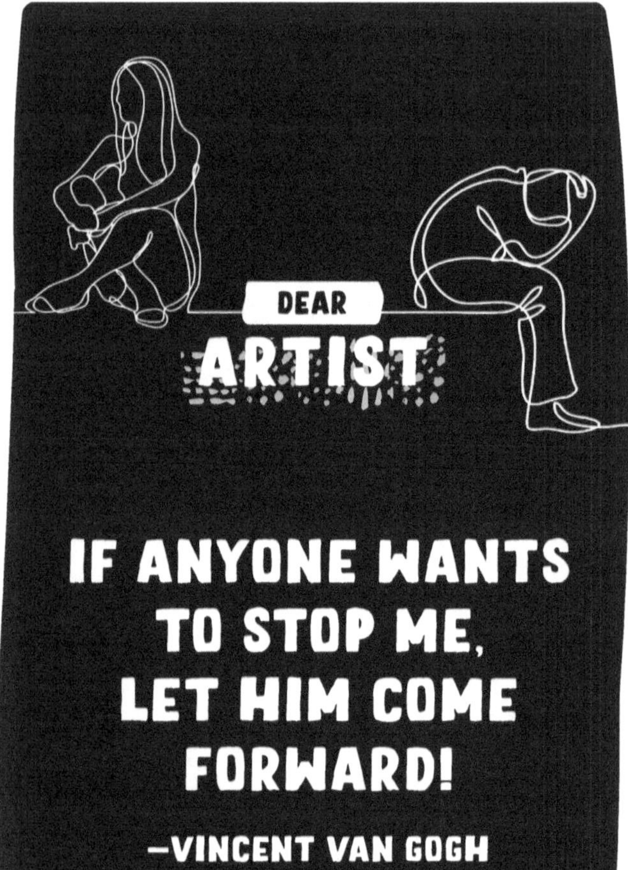

DEAR
ARTIST

IF ANYONE WANTS
TO STOP ME,
LET HIM COME
FORWARD!
—VINCENT VAN GOGH

DEAR ARTIST,

Reclaim a sense of wonder. Remember what it was like to be a child. In the days when you would wake up and decide "Today I am a dinosaur" or "Today I am building a spaceship." There was no question as to how that was going to happen or if the blankets you'd placed on the chairs were perfect for space travel. It was exciting!

"What could go here?"
"Ooo, you know what would be cool?"

The dining room was no longer where you ate dinner, it was now a planet full of little green men. No one hung out in the living room anymore, now that it had become a prehistoric jungle.

The blank page isn't something to be scared of or intimidated by. It's something to be excited and curious about.

What *could* happen? What new thing might you discover? The blank page is for you to try.

See if it leads somewhere. Who knows? It may illuminate some new incredible part of your soul you didn't even know was there, waiting to be discovered.

Art is play.
And play is serious business.
Learn to play again.

Reclaim the wonder of a child and your art will sparkle with the shine of possibility.

DEAR ARTIST,

I know you are wrestling with giving up. This life is just too hard. For years you've felt like you've been hanging on by a thread—a thread that could snap at any given moment.

If you make the wrong move, if you pull a little too hard, everything—yourself included—might collapse. Getting a "safe" job might kill your soul, but at least you could make the rent on time. At least all the looks would stop.

You'd no longer be the odd one out if you just fell back in line.

Just a reminder as you're wrestling with these thoughts: You didn't choose to be an artist.

Your craft, the instrument, the canvas, the stage, the page...

It chose you. The Universe detected something in you that the world needed to hear and see. You were chosen as a vessel to carry that message into the darkness of a dying world. Express the message that maybe only you have ears to hear.

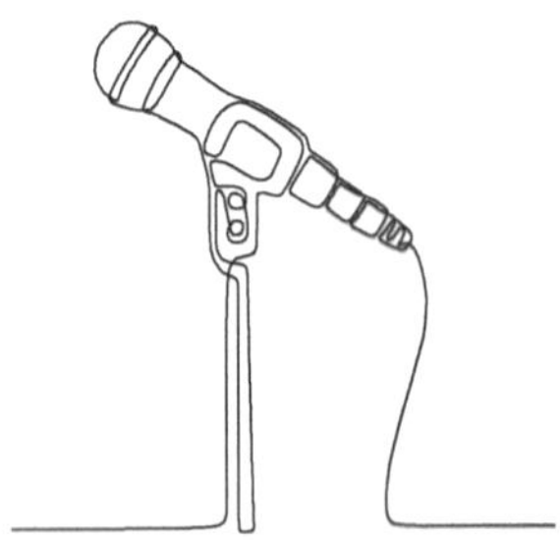

Redirection, sure. We all redirect at different moments in time.

But completely giving up? Holding a knife to the throat of the very thing that gives you life? Believe me, the day you give up is the day your life is over.

Then and only then.
Not today.
Not tomorrow.
Not when the panic rises in your soul.
Not when life is pitch dark and you don't know where to go.

Giving up on your art is tantamount to giving up on life.

Don't give up on life.

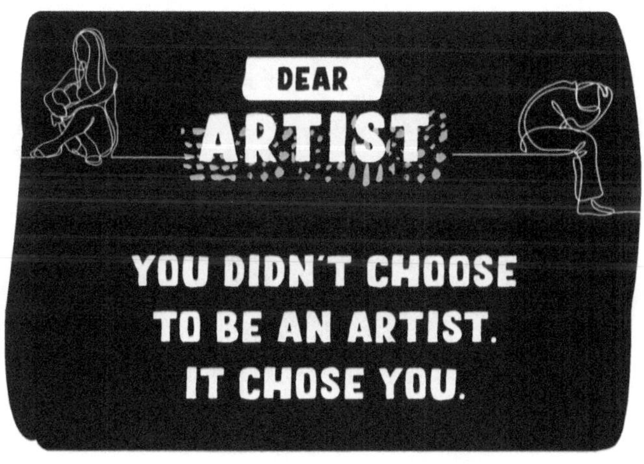

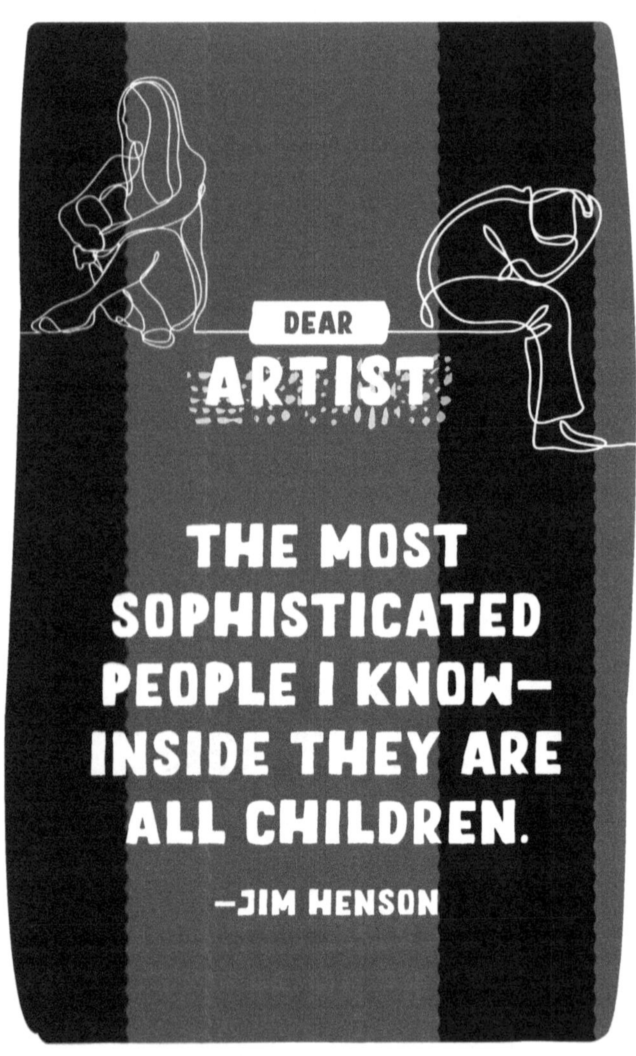
DEAR
ARTIST

THE MOST
SOPHISTICATED
PEOPLE I KNOW—
INSIDE THEY ARE
ALL CHILDREN.
—JIM HENSON

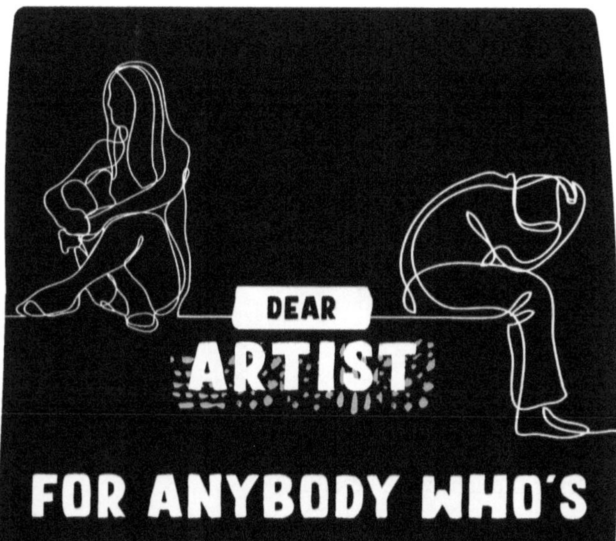

FOR ANYBODY WHO'S ON THE DOWNSIDE OF ADVANTAGE AND RELYING PURELY ON COURAGE... IT'S POSSIBLE.

—RUSSELL CROWE

DEAR ARTIST,

You don't need permission to do things. You don't need to wait for someone to come along and invite you on their journey.

Forge your own path. Invite others into your vision.
Leap your own hurdles rather than leaping someone else's.
Once you get to them, you'll find that they aren't as daunting (or often as hard) as you led yourself to believe.

Take chances.
Risk everything.

It's scary, but the rewards take you to higher heights than you ever thought were possible.

Be a pioneer of your own frontier.

Don't wait for the day where you have to say, "I wish."
Look at your life today and say, "I plan."

Write your own story.

And make it a good one.

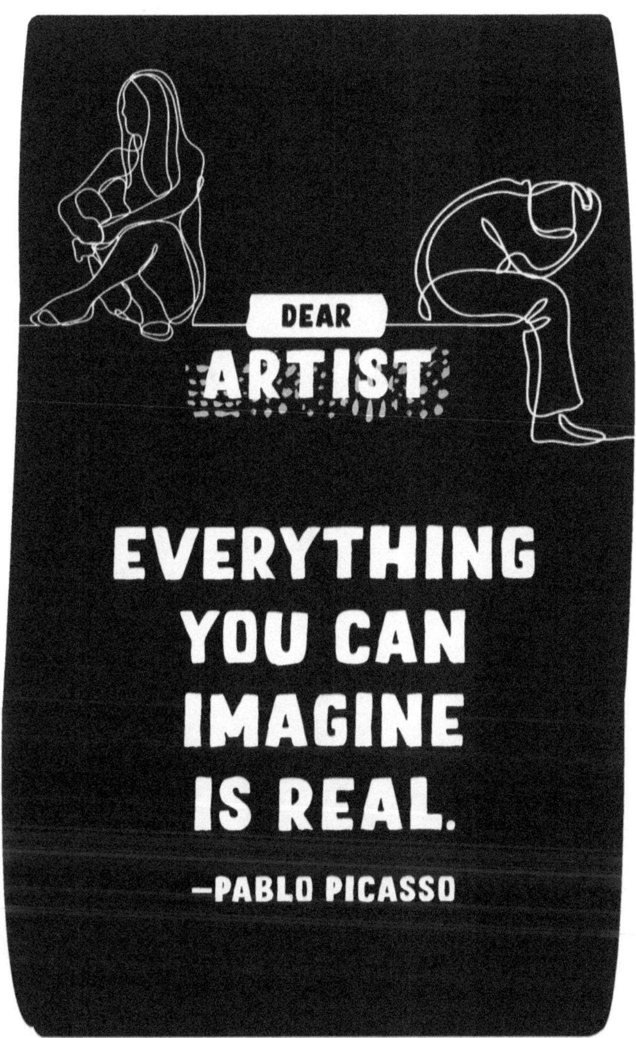
DEAR
ARTIST
EVERYTHING
YOU CAN
IMAGINE
IS REAL.
—PABLO PICASSO

DEAR ARTIST,

Every new day is an empty canvas, with your hand poised above the color tones of fear and doubt. But you also have a whole palate of other colors to choose from.

Hope.
Trust.
Faith.
Curiosity.
Discovery.

Dip your brush in a new color today.

There is a masterpiece waiting to be splashed across the page, if you only dare to follow your intuition.

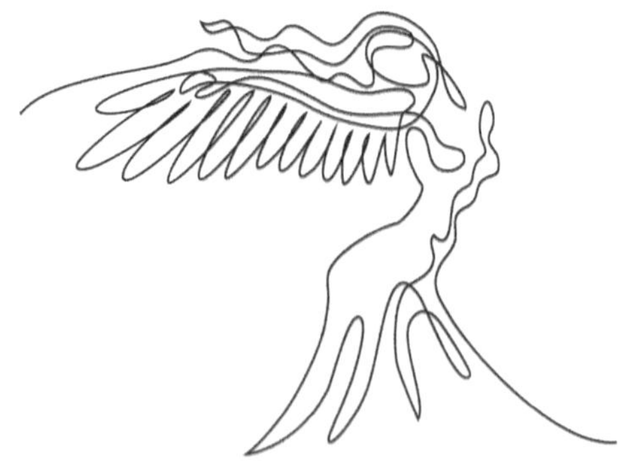

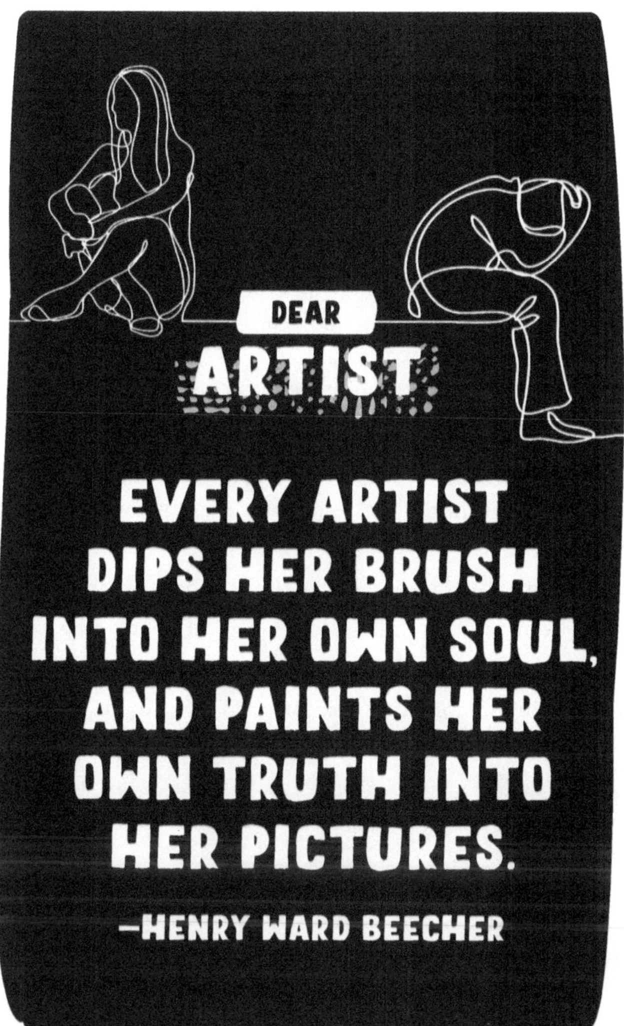
DEAR
ARTIST
EVERY ARTIST
DIPS HER BRUSH
INTO HER OWN SOUL,
AND PAINTS HER
OWN TRUTH INTO
HER PICTURES.
—HENRY WARD BEECHER

DEAR ARTIST,

Be careful who you share your hopes, dreams, and ventures with, even if they're good friends or family members. Oftentimes out of a sense of concern for our well-being, loved ones will try to reel us in from what they interpret to be a dangerous and uncertain path. While this is almost always done with the best of intentions, the last thing you need right now is someone telling you to be sensible and safe. Creativity is sensible. And being true to yourself and your happiness is the only path that's safe.

Keep an eye on the type of people you surround yourself with regularly. If they tend to constantly be cautioning you about "taking this thing a little too seriously"—whether outright or in subtle ways—perhaps it is time to take a step back and reevaluate the amount of time you are spending with them. This doesn't mean stop seeing or being friends with them entirely, but by confiding in them, you could subconsciously be reinforcing your own doubts and fears by listening to someone else put a voice to them. This just leads to self-sabotage down the road.

Your art, and the creation of it, is a vulnerable and sacred thing.

You don't need anyone trying to clip your wings while you are teaching yourself how to fly.

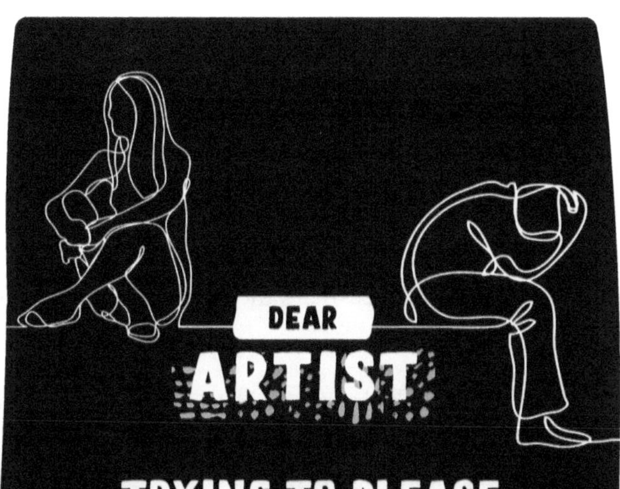

TRYING TO PLEASE
EVERYBODY IS IMPOSSIBLE.
IF YOU DID THAT, YOU'D END
UP IN THE MIDDLE WITH
NOBODY LIKING YOU. YOU'VE
GOT TO MAKE THE DECISION
ABOUT WHAT YOU THINK IS
YOUR BEST, AND DO IT.

—JOHN LENNON

DEAR ARTIST,

If you have something to say, but aren't sure how to say it, think about the mode in which it might best be expressed.

Does this idea need to be a book? A song? A scene? Would it be best expressed through a performance without words, like dance or even mime?

Don't think you need to stick to one artistic mode of expression simply because that's the one you know and are good at.

Regardless of the vehicle, if you have something burning in your heart that you feel needs to be said, then it is your duty and responsibility to say it.

To make it.

To do it.

The idea came to you for a reason. Follow it.

If it needs to be expressed in the way you feel it does, then the result will be exactly what it was supposed to be all along. Just create. Just do. Follow your intuition and manifest into existence what has been placed in your soul.

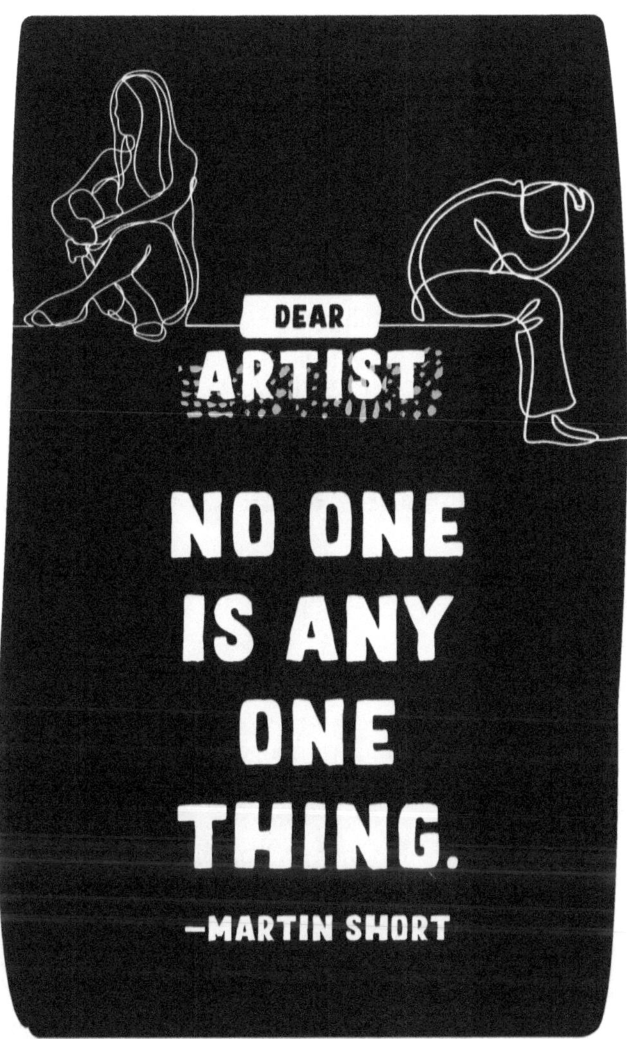
DEAR
ARTIST
NO ONE
IS ANY
ONE
THING.
—MARTIN SHORT

DEAR ARTIST,

Stop worrying about whether it's good or not.

Let me say that again.

Stop. Worrying. About. Whether. It's. Good. Or. Not.

Trying to be "good" is the death of imagination. Trying to be "good" is the death of creativity. If you are so hyper-focused on only doing "good" work, you lose the vast, beautiful world of possibility and exploration. And if you've lost that, you've lost the golden nuggets of truth that often reveal themselves through our falsely labeled "mistakes".

The goal is to be honest. Try to find that nugget of truth in yourself and express it through whatever medium is your own.

A lyric.
A brushstroke.
An emotional moment.

Always give it everything you've got and do the absolute best you can, but stop trying to control the outcome.

Stop trying to be good. Be honest. Do your best. And let it be.

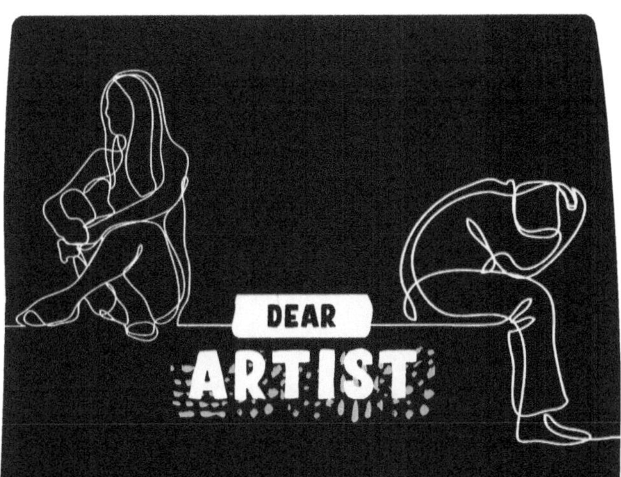

TRYING TO BE GOOD IS THE KISS OF DEATH. TRY TO BE HONEST. TRY TO BE TRUTHFUL IN YOUR WORK, IN YOUR LIFE. IT'S WHAT I ADMIRE MOST WHEN I SEE ACTING THAT SPEAKS TO ME OR MOVES ME, WHEN I FEEL THERE IS JUST SEARING HONESTY.

—SARAH PAULSON

DEAR ARTIST,

Don't pretend to have all the answers. In fact, it's far preferable if you don't. Because here's a little secret; none of us know what we're doing. All we have is the experience we've gained so far, and our instinct in *this* moment.

Ask questions and admit when you don't know. Your first question will lead to another question which will lead to three more.

The artist's life is an endless frontier of questions and discoveries.

Not a single one of us is qualified. No one's instincts are greater than yours, and your instincts are no greater than anyone else's. There are simply our instincts. Follow them. They know the way.

It's okay to not know.

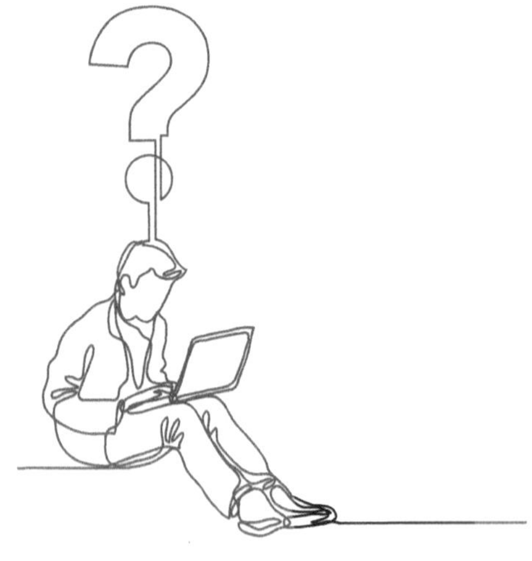

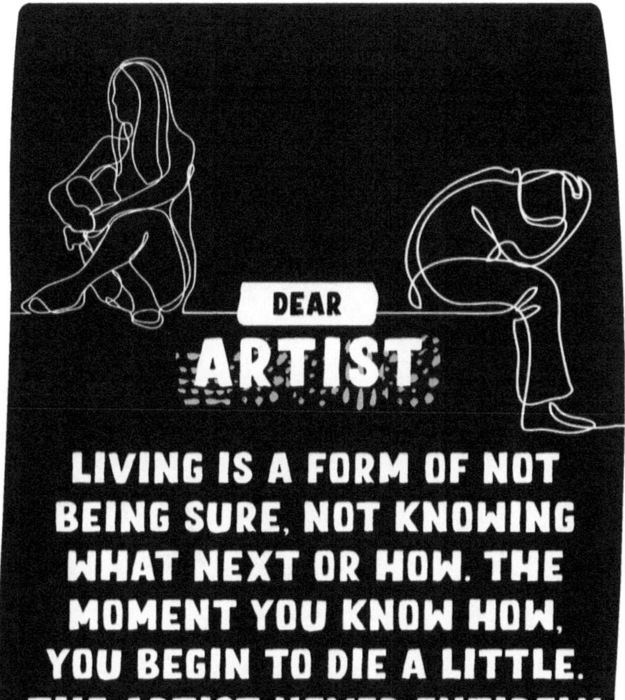

LIVING IS A FORM OF NOT BEING SURE, NOT KNOWING WHAT NEXT OR HOW. THE MOMENT YOU KNOW HOW, YOU BEGIN TO DIE A LITTLE. THE ARTIST NEVER ENTIRELY KNOWS. WE GUESS. WE MAY BE WRONG, BUT WE TAKE LEAP AFTER LEAP IN THE DARK.

—AGNES DE MILLE

DEAR ARTIST,

Close your eyes.

Deep breath.

Feel that?

That's life.

Open your eyes.

You have today.

Go.

Live.

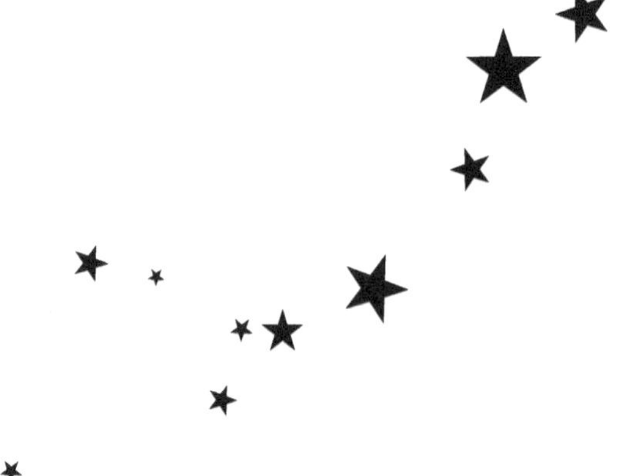

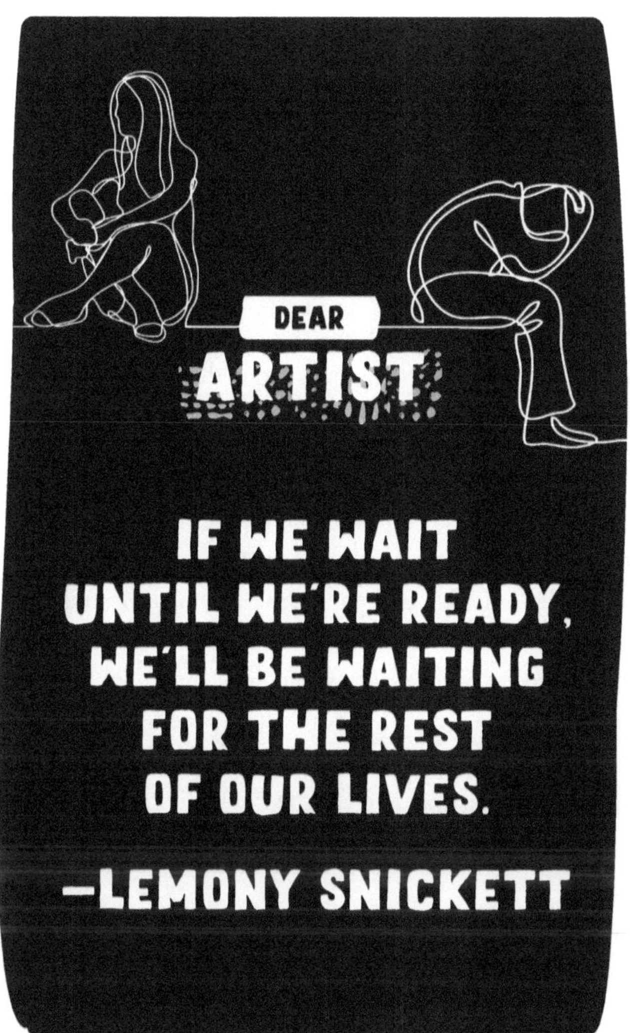

DEAR
ARTIST
IF WE WAIT
UNTIL WE'RE READY,
WE'LL BE WAITING
FOR THE REST
OF OUR LIVES.
—LEMONY SNICKETT

DEAR ARTIST,

Every once in a while, show the world a piece of your work that's not perfect. It's important to talk about and see one another's best efforts, even if it isn't quite up to par with what we envisioned.

An audition where you flubbed a line, a painting that didn't turn out quite as you wanted, a third draft that is still rough around the edges.

It's important to show these things every so often because there are so many young artists out there who don't even have the courage to begin.

If all they see are the flawless masterpieces that we so carefully choose to put out into the world, there is a tendency to believe that from the get-go, they must also be perfect. This belief is false. Let them see that you make mistakes. Let them see that it doesn't all just come together. Let them see that there is a process of trial and error that every artist goes through. If we can pull back the curtain enough to let them in on this little secret, we might be able to help break down their fear of starting, and their fear of failing.

Show your brushstrokes. Every so often, let the world see.

And in doing so, you may just give someone the invitation they need to begin.

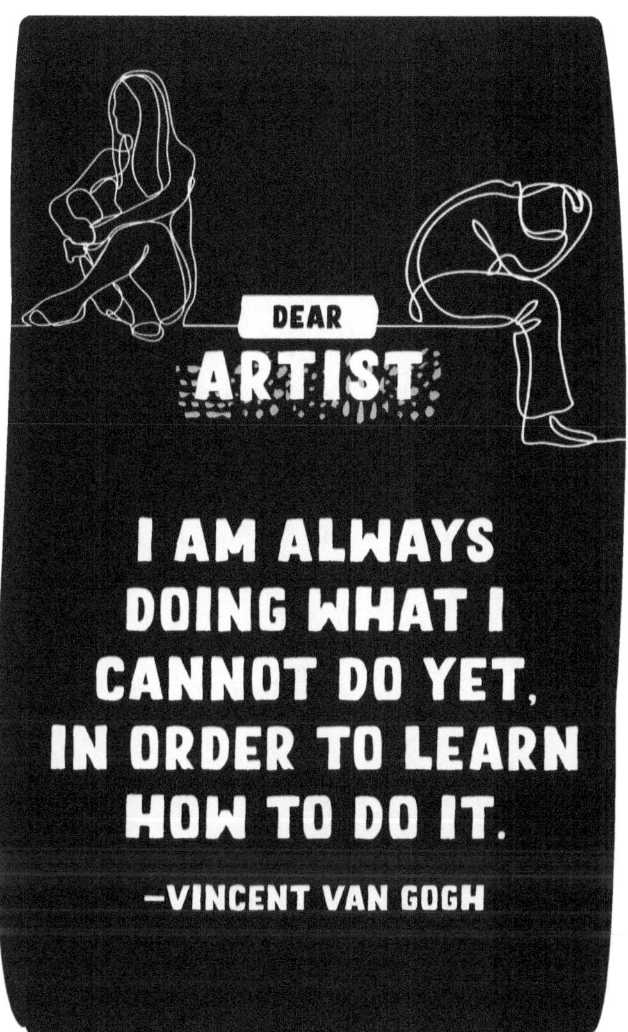

DEAR
ARTIST
I AM ALWAYS DOING WHAT I CANNOT DO YET, IN ORDER TO LEARN HOW TO DO IT.
—VINCENT VAN GOGH

DEAR ARTIST,

Your mind is running wild with possibilities, and not in a good way. You woke up today just knowing you will never make it and this was all for nothing and now you're lost and you're going to look like an idiot and you've been bad all along and you've just been making a fool out of yourself and and AND ...

Stop.
Breathe.
Come back to center.
Silence the swirling thoughts in your head.

You have this moment, right here, right now. The past is irrelevant and the future is out of your control. What you can control is this next moment in front of you.

How are you going to use it?

What are you going to do ... *now*?

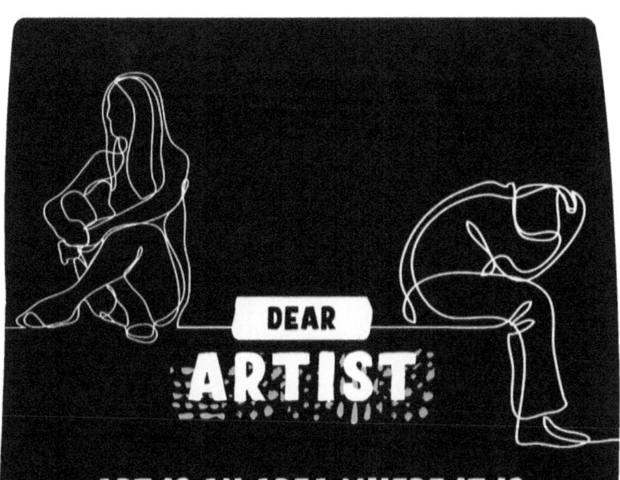

ART IS AN AREA WHERE IT IS IMPOSSIBLE TO WALK WITHOUT STUMBLING. THERE ARE IN STORE FOR YOU MANY UNSUCCESSFUL DAYS AND WHOLE UNSUCCESSFUL SEASONS: THERE WILL BE GREAT MISUNDERSTANDINGS AND DEEP DISAPPOINTMENTS... YOU MUST BE PREPARED FOR ALL THIS, ACCEPT IT AND NEVERTHELESS, STUBBORNLY, FANATICALLY FOLLOW YOUR OWN WAY.

—ANTON CHEKHOV

DEAR ARTIST,

You've got the desire. You know you *want* to do this, you just don't know if you can. Everything in you says maybe, just *maybe*, you've got what it takes. That this time it might work. But you've had this feeling before. You made a fool of yourself last time, what makes you think it won't happen again?

Remind me … who are you doing this for?

By whose definition are you considered a fool?

All artists take sloppy steps. The mess is necessary. You can't go from first toddle to Olympic runner without something in between.

Those wobbly stumbles are necessary and good and should be applauded. There is no shame in them.

You don't have to vanquish all fear before you step out.

Stop shaming yourself for your valiance to try.

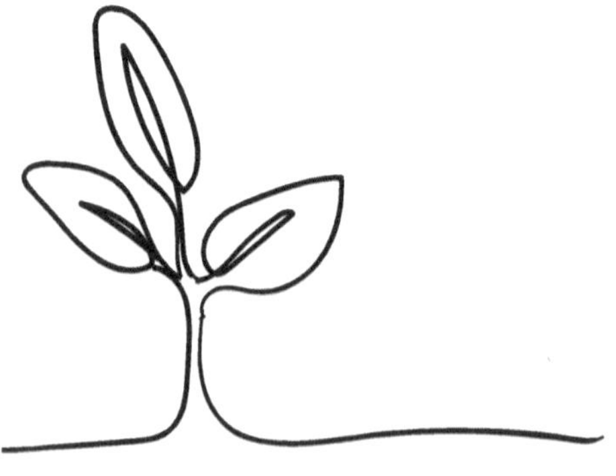

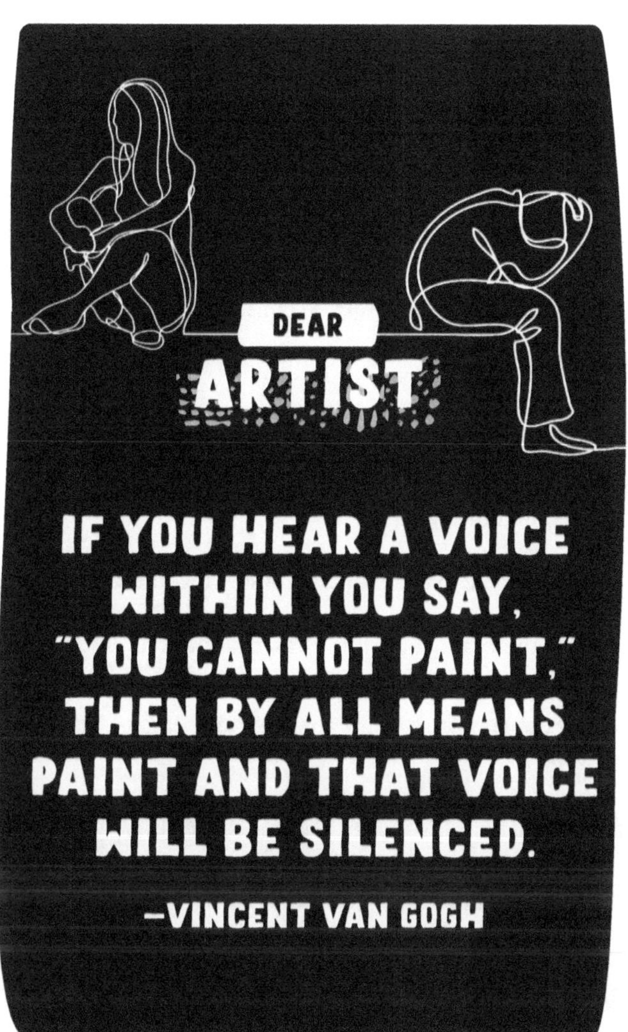
DEAR
ARTIST
IF YOU HEAR A VOICE
WITHIN YOU SAY,
"YOU CANNOT PAINT,"
THEN BY ALL MEANS
PAINT AND THAT VOICE
WILL BE SILENCED.
–VINCENT VAN GOGH

DEAR ARTIST,

Quiet your soul and wait for inspiration. So often we feel as though we have to be working on something every second of the day, and get caught up in a whirlwind of our own making. A spinning cyclone of false productivity. We frantically try to come up with something—anything—because we subconsciously believe that inaction is a form of laziness, and that in order to look ourselves in the mirror and call ourselves an artist, we must be constantly producing.

This is not so.

One inspired thought,
one inspired brushstroke,
one inspired motion

is more valuable than a thousand hastily manufactured ideas.

I know there are such things as deadlines and sometimes you just have to get something down. But as often as you can, wait. Stay still. With the eyes and ears of your heart wide open.

That small guiding voice is always speaking. Always. Yet sometimes it's wisdom is hardly more than a whisper. Learn to turn down the volume of your soul far enough to hear it.

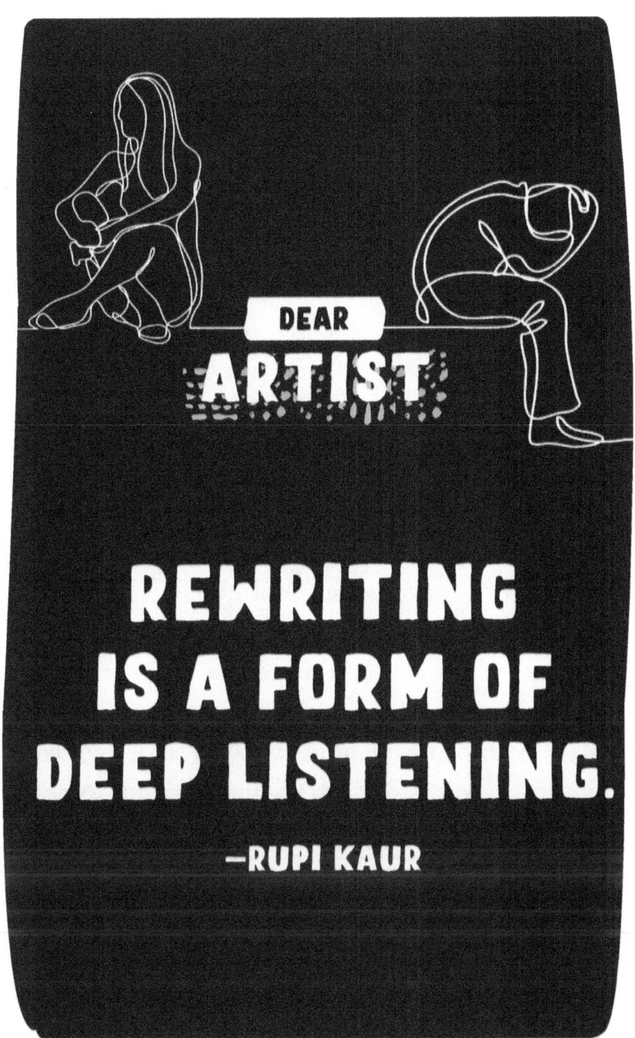

DEAR
ARTIST

REWRITING
IS A FORM OF
DEEP LISTENING.
—RUPI KAUR

DEAR ARTIST,

What is it that so captures the artist's soul about beauty? The things that make us catch our breath. Whether it is a view, a melody, the swirling of colors on a canvas, the perfect placement of words and lyrics that flow just so ... Artists are obsessed with beauty. Humans are obsessed with beauty. The sound of music, the smell of fresh-cut grass, the Colorado mountains on a crisp November day, the perfect conduit for expressing deep feelings and emotions. Why are we so captivated by it? This flow of emotional expression that reaches out to trace the soul like the grazing finger of a lover.

You can't put words to it—the beauty of beauty. When a ballad plays and you can't help but dance. When you are unafraid to shout your song from the rooftops of who you are. Beauty is mysterious. And I think if we were able to explain it or figure out the formula for what makes something truly beautiful, it would lose its luster. The very thing that made us catch our breath would be rendered ordinary. Beauty isn't meant to be explained. It's not meant to be debated or picked apart. Beauty is meant to be felt. Experienced. So feel it.

Savor the beauty of your human experience. And savor the beauty of the broken poem that your soul is writing.

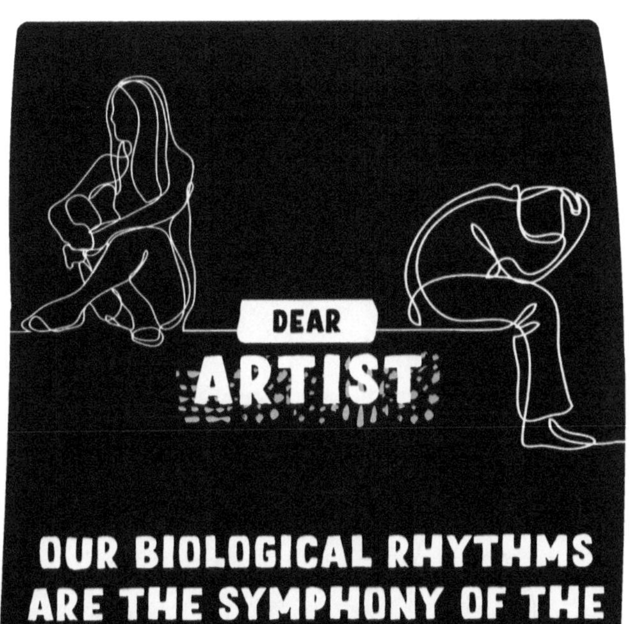

OUR BIOLOGICAL RHYTHMS ARE THE SYMPHONY OF THE COSMOS, MUSIC EMBEDDED DEEP WITHIN US TO WHICH WE DANCE, EVEN WHEN WE CAN'T NAME THE TUNE.

—DEEPAK CHOPRA

DEAR ARTIST,

The greatest risk you'll ever take

is when you choose

to play it safe.

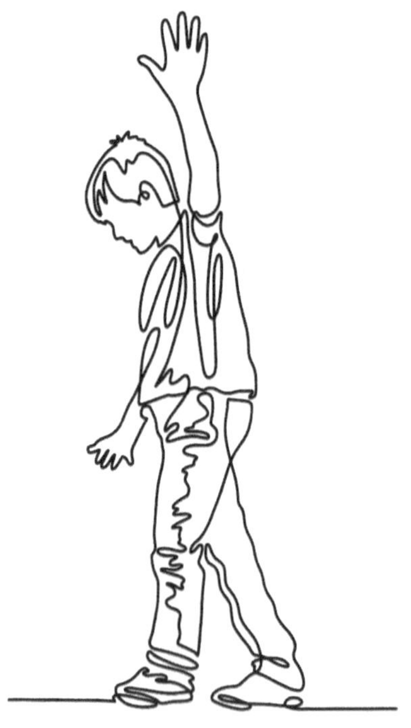

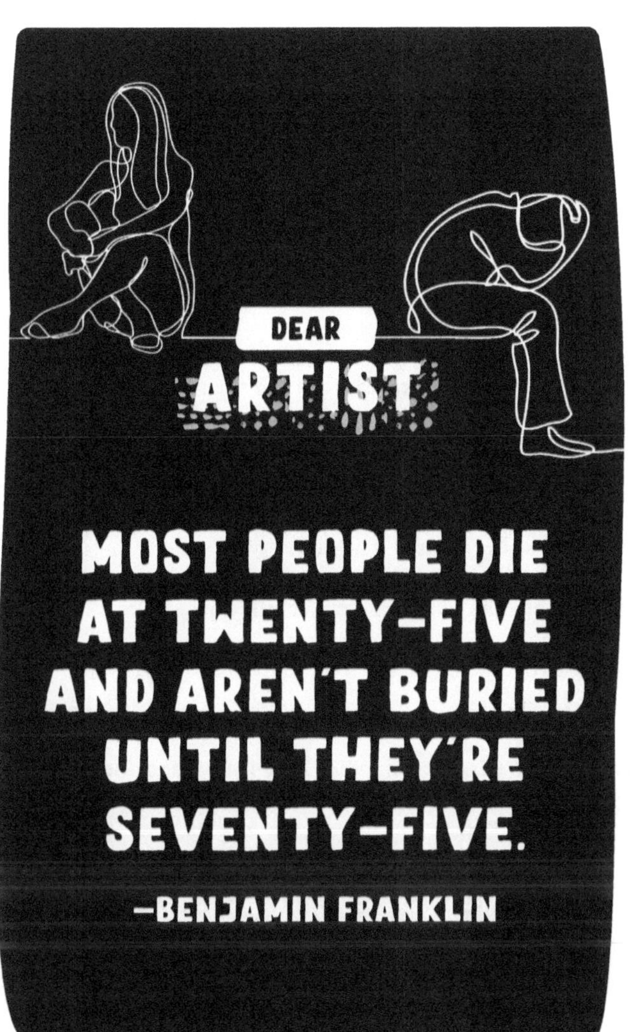
DEAR
ARTIST

MOST PEOPLE DIE
AT TWENTY-FIVE
AND AREN'T BURIED
UNTIL THEY'RE
SEVENTY-FIVE.

-BENJAMIN FRANKLIN

DEAR ARTIST,

It didn't work. And that's okay. You failed. Alright. Now what? Things didn't go according to plan. They almost never do. And yet, you wanted this so badly. You *needed* this so badly.

What do you do when you are, once again, looking down at all the shattered pieces of your dreams… A creative miscarriage that you cared for and nurtured for so long.

You weep.

You know all the platitudes, all the sayings.

"The tears you cry today water the seeds of tomorrow."
"This just means there's something better on the way."

But you know what? Fuck that.

This meant the world to you. It still does.

Maybe there's some way you can still salvage some of the broken bits…

Maybe there is. And maybe there isn't. That doesn't matter right now.

You will be strong enough to sort through the pieces in time. I promise. Eventually, you will gather up the courage to begin again.

For now, just weep.

Feel the depth of your grief. Allow it to run its course.

And in doing so, experience sorrow's cleansing.

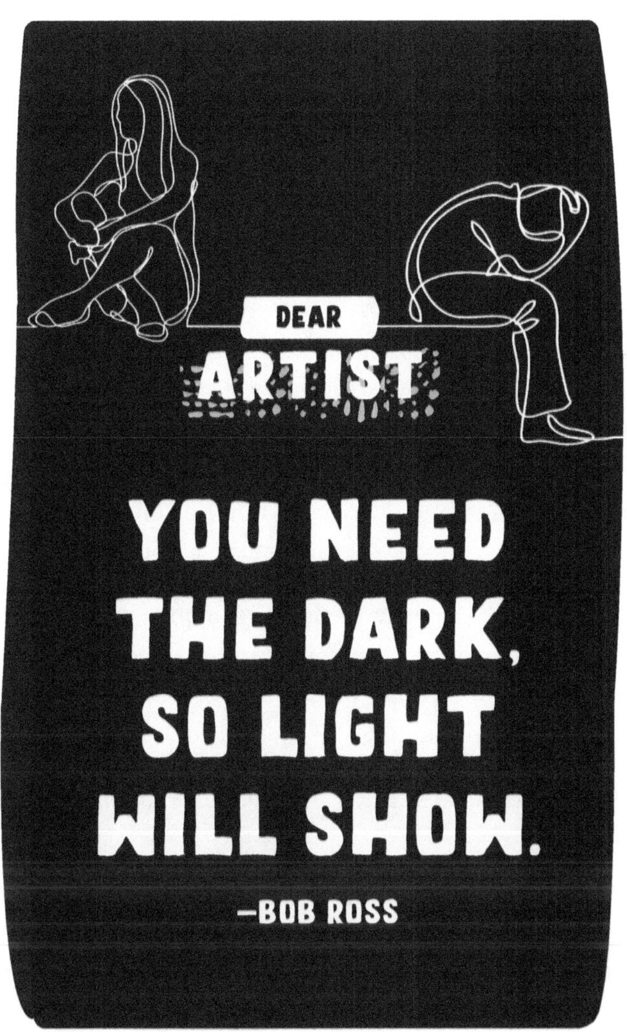

DEAR
ARTIST

YOU NEED
THE DARK,
SO LIGHT
WILL SHOW.
—BOB ROSS

DEAR ARTIST,

Don't be afraid of your own evolution.

We are always learning and changing. Something we believe to be true today, we may find out is totally false tomorrow. Don't dread or be afraid of this. Welcome it. An artist's life is a series of creative hypotheses.

If you have certain ideas about your art—you have to "make it" in *this* way, or *that* style would never work for you, or you only use *this* particular method—and you find your thoughts changing on the subject, roll with it. The moment we accept the fact that we never stop learning, growing, and evolving, we open ourselves up to an entirely new world of possibilities. And that releases us from the intense pressure of our own narrowly held requirements for ourselves.

The artist's life is an ever-changing improv game. There is always something new to be learned, some fresh bit of information to be applied. Don't cling to old beliefs just because they are familiar. "Yes, And" them.

As an artist and a human, it is something to be embraced.

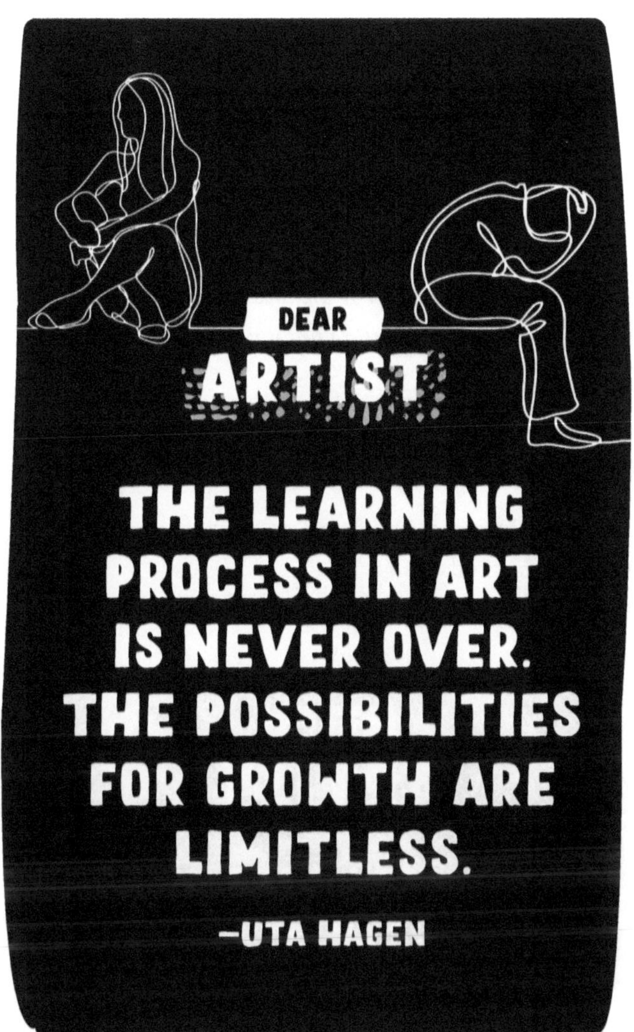
DEAR
ARTIST
THE LEARNING PROCESS IN ART IS NEVER OVER. THE POSSIBILITIES FOR GROWTH ARE LIMITLESS.
—UTA HAGEN

DEAR ARTIST,

It's interesting when you think about faith. Faith in your work. Faith that you will someday make a living as an artist. Faith in that little voice guiding you, always to the very next thing.

You find yourself constantly afraid of that voice going away.

What if it doesn't show up this time?
What if I'm too wound up or anxious to hear it?
What if I've never heard it, to begin with?

What if, what if, what if...

Stop living in the what-ifs.

Has your compass ever failed to point you north? Why would it start today?

Let me be very clear about one thing; This faith we're talking about is not religious. Far from it. Contrary to popular belief, there is no particular set of rules or school of thought you must adhere to in order to be a person of faith.

What we're talking about is a belief in knowledge.

That the same thing that has led you to this point will be there to continue leading you tomorrow, and next week, and next year.

It can be nerve-wracking having to operate in faith, because you've felt so let down by it in the past. But you've actually got evidence this time. You're always shown the next step.

Just the step, not the staircase.

I don't know how it works, and sometimes I don't know that I want to. Call it intuition, the Universe, a gut feeling or God—but your compass knows where it's pointing you. All that remains is whether you will listen and follow where it leads.

Sometimes all we have to go on is faith.

And sometimes faith is enough.

DEAR ARTIST,

Comparing yourself to other artists is a completely fruitless endeavor. Art is not like a sport. It's not like a campaign. It's not like an equation. There are no numbers to run.

Art is an expression.

An expression cannot be measured.

Art cannot be measured.

I see this all the time in the audition room. As soon as someone walks in the door that you think looks better than you, or is sporting your same style, or whose wardrobe fits the character better, the thoughts start running rampant.

Oh, we were supposed to dress casual… I guess I'm not getting this role.

That person just exudes confidence… I might as well just go home now.

All of these other people look like better versions of me… Why embarrass myself by going in at all?

Listen to me closely. Someone could walk in the room and look exactly like you, down to the shoes you are wearing and they still aren't going to give the same performance you are.

Because art is about expression.

No one has your same point of view. No one's movements are exactly like yours. No one phrases and mixes words in the exact same way you do.

One is not better. One is not worse. They are simply different.

There is not a single person to compare to because there is not a single person exactly like you. The only person you're competing with is yourself.

Set the bar high, but remember, you're only trying to reach your new personal best.

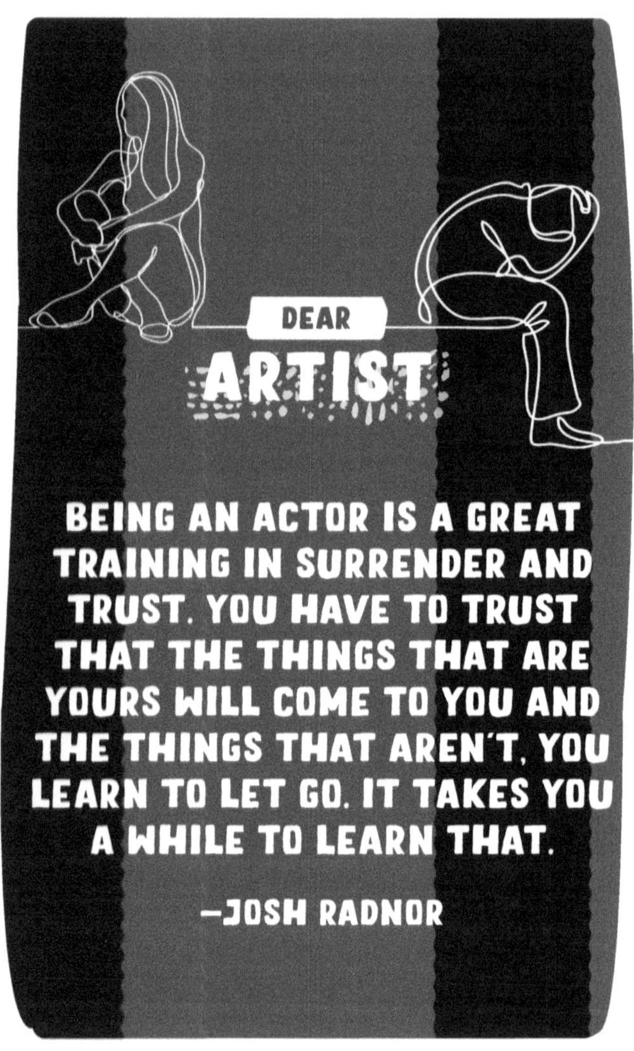
DEAR
ARTIST

BEING AN ACTOR IS A GREAT TRAINING IN SURRENDER AND TRUST. YOU HAVE TO TRUST THAT THE THINGS THAT ARE YOURS WILL COME TO YOU AND THE THINGS THAT AREN'T, YOU LEARN TO LET GO. IT TAKES YOU A WHILE TO LEARN THAT.

—JOSH RADNOR

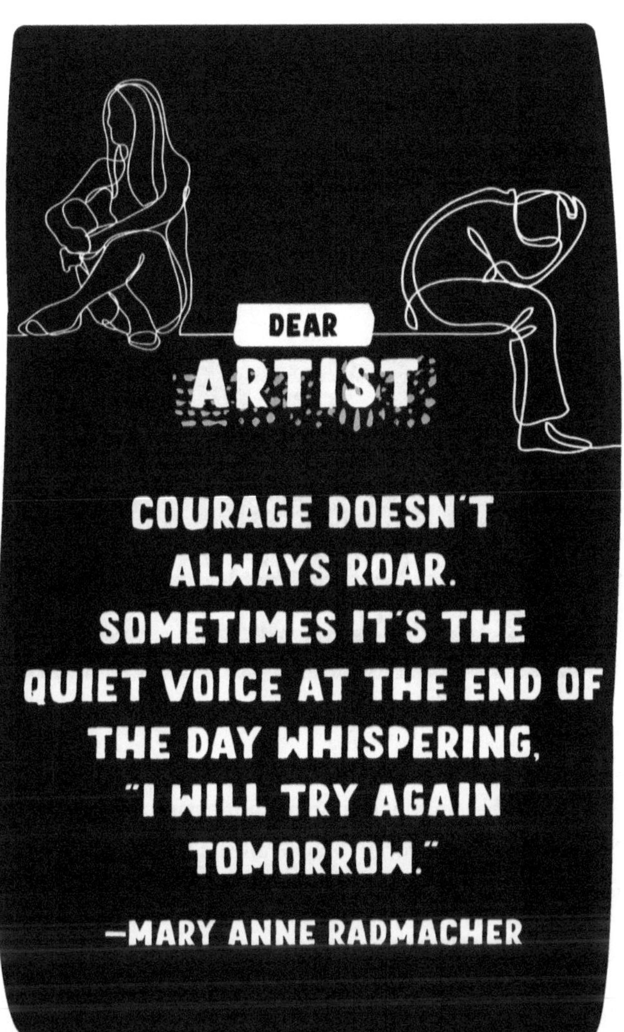

DEAR
ARTIST

COURAGE DOESN'T
ALWAYS ROAR.
SOMETIMES IT'S THE
QUIET VOICE AT THE END OF
THE DAY WHISPERING,
"I WILL TRY AGAIN
TOMORROW."

—MARY ANNE RADMACHER

DEAR ARTIST,

Do you find yourself feeling bad whenever you go into a venue dedicated to your art form? A theater, a gallery… Even a library or an art center? You may not talk about it, you may not even admit it to yourself, but it's there. Nagging. Always playing at the back of your mind, even as you enjoy other's work.

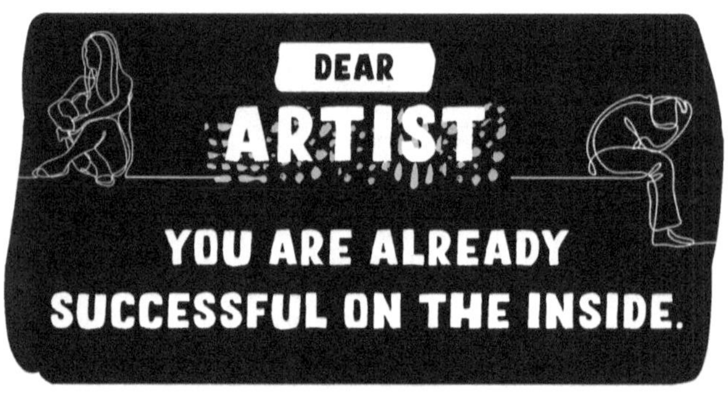

You're not up there. Your work isn't displayed among theirs. Will it ever be? So much time has gone past. Have you been doing something wrong? Maybe all the right steps just add up to a whole lot of nothing.

You feel like smoke, slowly fading into the wind.

Or maybe not so slowly.

Begin to change perspectives.

Stop thinking about where you're not. What you don't have. What your life isn't.

Every time you look at a painting, or see a performance, or crack open a book, see yourself in that work. Say to yourself,

That is me up there.

Because guess what? It will be. You are simply affirming what's already true. Your future is not some mythical creature that will never arrive.

You are already successful on the inside.

Remind yourself of this truth until the physical world echoes in response.

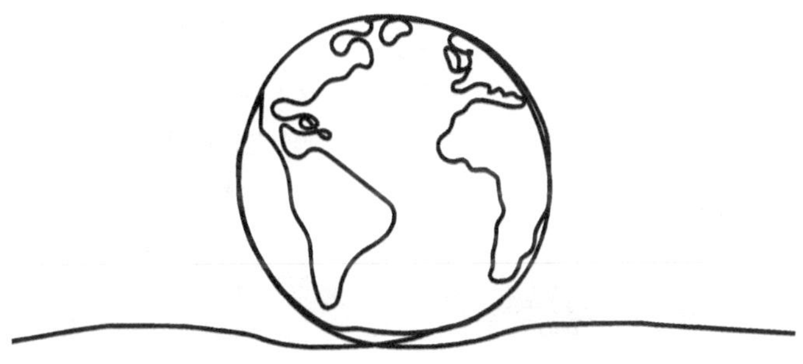

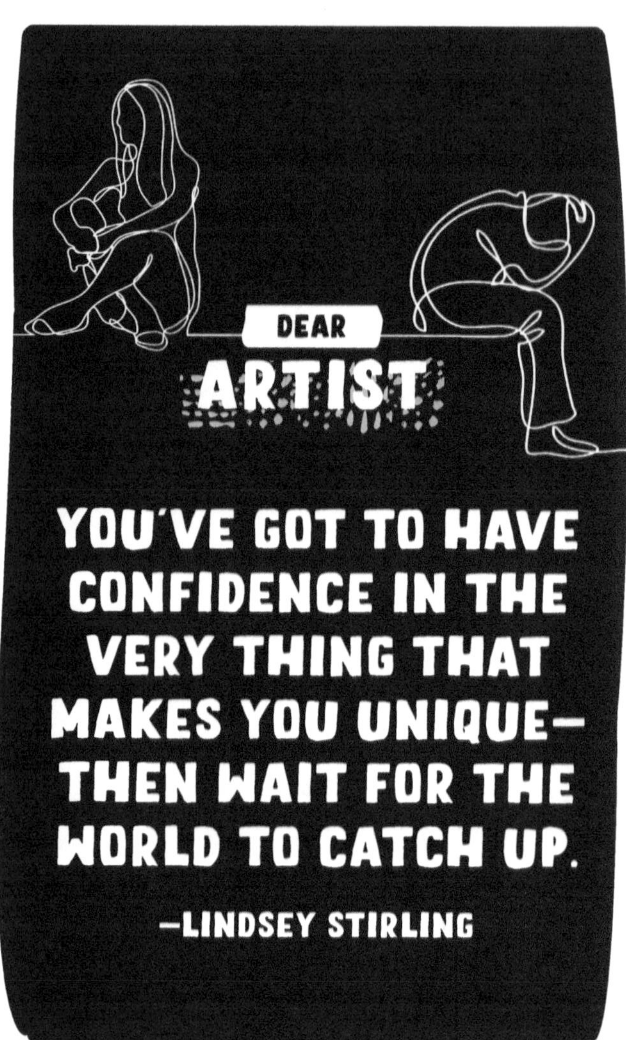
DEAR
ARTIST
YOU'VE GOT TO HAVE CONFIDENCE IN THE VERY THING THAT MAKES YOU UNIQUE—THEN WAIT FOR THE WORLD TO CATCH UP.
—LINDSEY STIRLING

DEAR ARTIST,

Living a different kind of life and doing a different kind of work does not make you lazy. Far from it.

Our job is to study the human condition. We are lucky enough to have access to places that others are not willing, or not able, to go. These realms are often uncomfortable, and can even at times be painful.

But into the shadows we dive. We seek the truth that is buried there, and it is our job to come back to the light and share with the world what we have found.

Mountains are scaled in our minds. Entire continents crossed in a spiritual realm. What we do is a service to the human race.

Don't make the mistake of believing anyone who shames you because your life looks different than theirs.

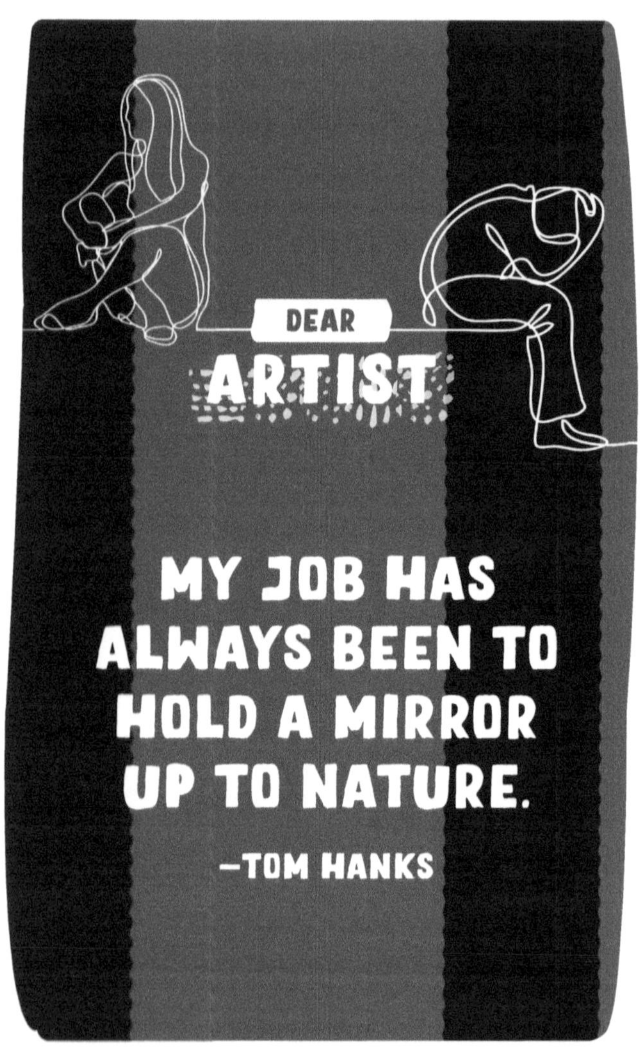
DEAR
ARTIST

MY JOB HAS
ALWAYS BEEN TO
HOLD A MIRROR
UP TO NATURE.
—TOM HANKS

DEAR ARTIST,

You are right on the brink of a breakthrough. The last mile of the race is always the hardest one to complete.

The home stretch is always the most enticing time to call it quits. Especially when you don't know how long the home stretch will last, or if you're even in the home stretch at all.

Too many people give up just as they are about to break through to the other side, and they never even know it.

You are right outside the door, my friend.

Don't be the one that gives up just before you see the light.

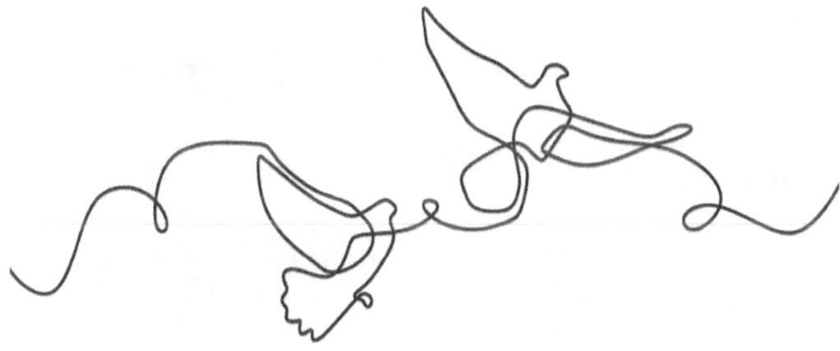

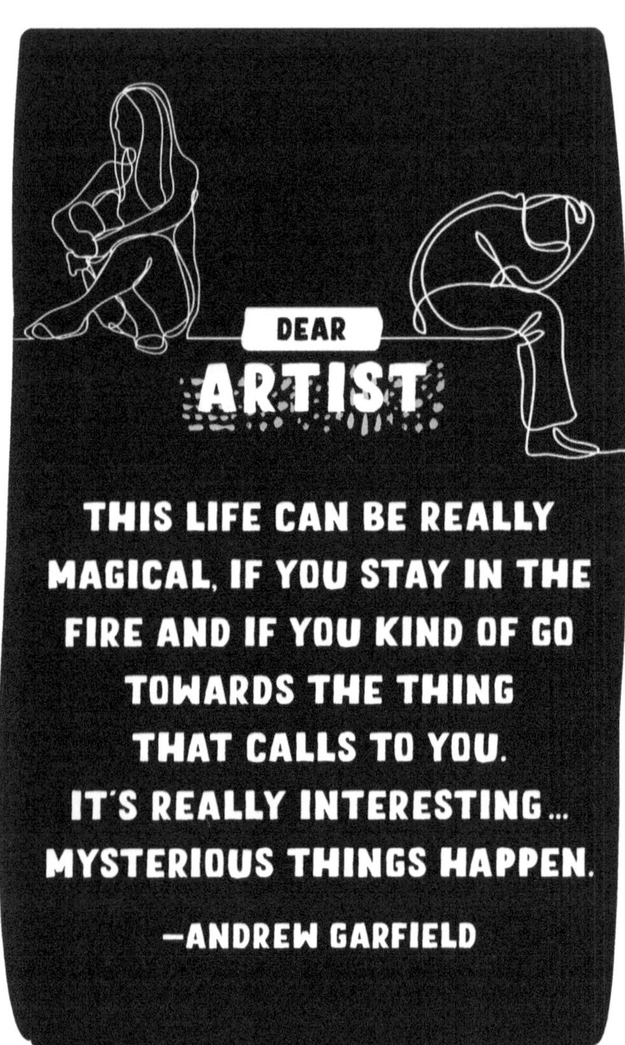
DEAR
ARTIST

THIS LIFE CAN BE REALLY
MAGICAL, IF YOU STAY IN THE
FIRE AND IF YOU KIND OF GO
TOWARDS THE THING
THAT CALLS TO YOU.
IT'S REALLY INTERESTING...
MYSTERIOUS THINGS HAPPEN.

—ANDREW GARFIELD

DEAR ARTIST,

You have a 6th sense that precious few could ever see. The vision you hold is something the rest of the world is often blind to.

So of course they mock and ridicule (intentionally or not).

They look and there's nothing there. They cannot see what you see, they cannot feel what you feel.

But just because they are blind to your vision, doesn't mean that what you see is not there.

An artist's vision is rarely validated until there is some tangible proof of its existence.

Remember this as you move about in the world before you have "made it." The chasm of time between the birth of an idea and the holding of the finished product in your hand is vast. Don't wait for their validation to give you permission to validate yourself. Your vision is as concrete and real right now as it will be on the day the world stands in awe. Don't get discouraged because they give you pitying looks.

They cannot see the beauty that you are so drawn to.

The beauty you'll charge through hell or high water just to be near.

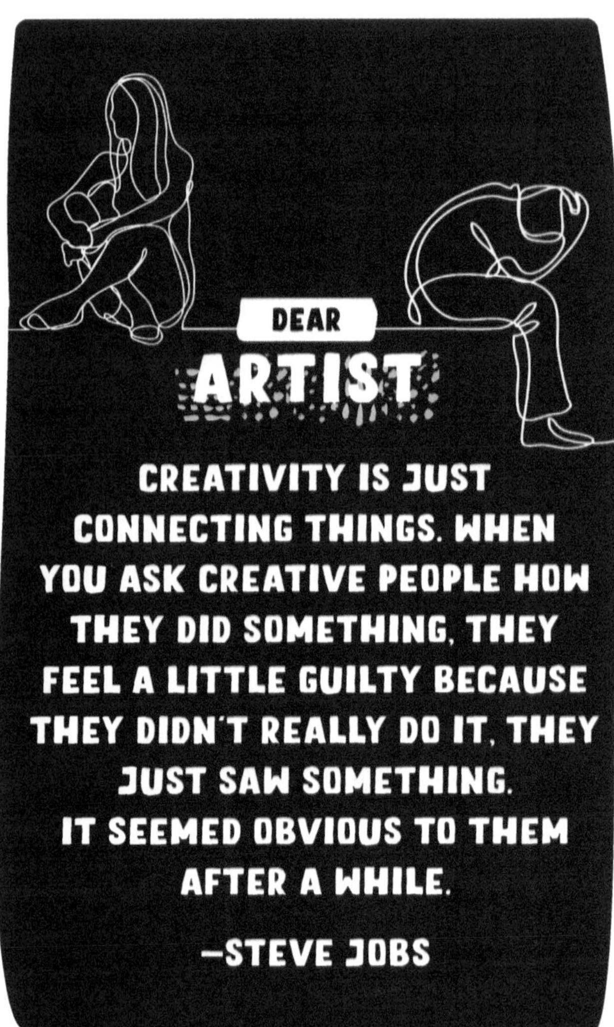

DEAR
ARTIST
CREATIVITY IS JUST CONNECTING THINGS. WHEN YOU ASK CREATIVE PEOPLE HOW THEY DID SOMETHING, THEY FEEL A LITTLE GUILTY BECAUSE THEY DIDN'T REALLY DO IT, THEY JUST SAW SOMETHING.
IT SEEMED OBVIOUS TO THEM AFTER A WHILE.
—STEVE JOBS

DEAR ARTIST,

Our lives tend to be ones of solitude. It is how we are built. Sometimes we become this way by choice, but often we seclude ourselves because we feel misunderstood.

You will be misunderstood. That is a guarantee. Friends, family, people you admire… Often it's the ones closest to us that seem to understand the least.

But being misunderstood doesn't have to be the tragedy it so often has the reputation of being.

Every person who has truly done something in this world has been misunderstood. The greatest humans in history have always been the odd man out. And if you look at those great stories that people love so much—the ones we go back to time and time again—it is almost universally recognized that being misunderstood is a sure sign that you're on the right path.

Does this make the confused questions and looks of pity any easier? No.

But it does give us weirdos a bit of comfort, now doesn't it?

If you're misunderstood, know that you're in good company. And that in being considered "weird" or "strange," you have a much higher chance of doing something truly remarkable.

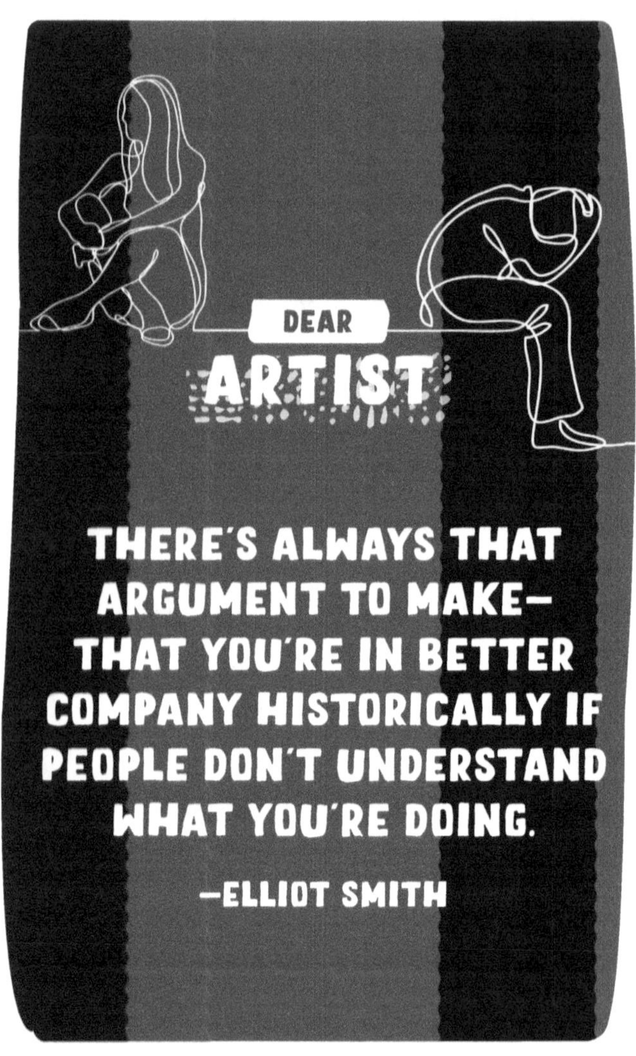

DEAR
ARTIST

THERE'S ALWAYS THAT
ARGUMENT TO MAKE—
THAT YOU'RE IN BETTER
COMPANY HISTORICALLY IF
PEOPLE DON'T UNDERSTAND
WHAT YOU'RE DOING.

—ELLIOT SMITH

DEAR ARTIST,

There is a passion that visits in the small hours of the morning. Like the spirit of a dove, it settles when you least expect it.

The world can be falling down around you and your worries still be strong, but in that silent moment, everything is okay.

Step outside, even in the darkest hours of the night, and listen. There is beauty found in silence.

There is healing found in stillness.

Consciously take time to immerse yourself in silence.

Listen to its voice. The healing that stillness brings is one of the most mysterious things I've ever encountered. But somehow, it knows how to mend. To stitch up.

There are things that the Universe is trying to say to you that can only be communicated through tranquility. For your soul's sake, listen. There is so much to be heard. So much to be healed.

Sit.
Listen.
Meditate.
Pray.

Allow your soul to be repaired in the sacred stillness of silence.

DEAR ARTIST,

I understand how miserable you are. Working a soul-crushing job that you hate, living in a city that always feels like it's closing in on you, scrolling through feeds that make you feel less than …

There are a thousand daily things that seem to drain you. At the end of it all, the last thing you want to do is put any effort into the things that used to make you shine.

An audition can feel hopeless if you know you're not going to get the part anyway, so why bother preparing it? That guitar is just a symbol of how far removed you are from your goals. Opening your computer just reveals a taunting cursor, mocking you as it blinks on an empty page.

No one told you it would be like this when you set out to follow your dreams.

Remember that this phase in life is a stepping stone. A page out of your book. A dark page, yes. But a page nonetheless. At the risk of sounding trite, there is so much more to your story.

From this stepping stone you will jump to another stepping stone, and then another. That roommate that you can't stand, their lease is just about up. That horrible job that you find yourself dreading every day, that is going to pay for the class that might open the door for your big break.

All storms run out of rain. And I promise that yours will too. Pull out an umbrella, or let it soak you to the bone, either one is fine. Do what you need to do. But this will eventually come to an end.

I need you to hold on until then.

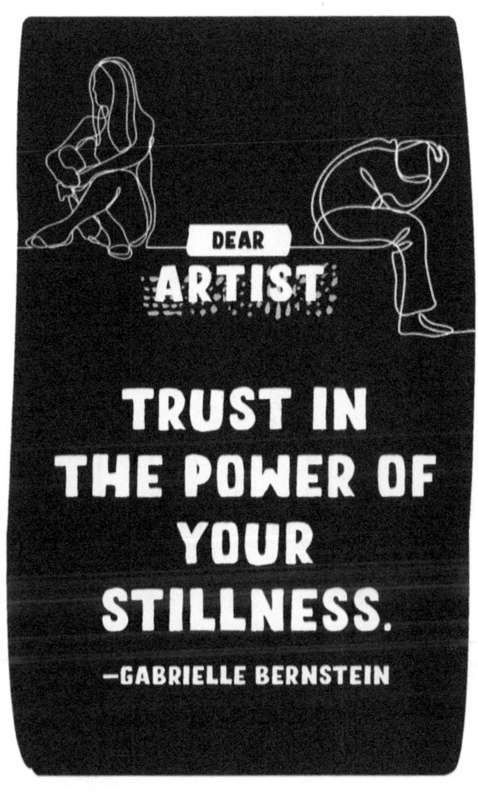

DEAR ARTIST,

Take small steps. Small steps become medium steps, which become bigger steps, which become giant steps. Sometimes you will take a smaller step after a big one. That's okay. A smaller step is still a step. Giant leaps cannot be made without baby shuffles behind them. The small steps are necessary and good, and exciting! They prove you're going in the right direction and act as markers of all your good progress.

You did well today. I'm proud of you. Get some rest. Your art will awaken with the dawn.

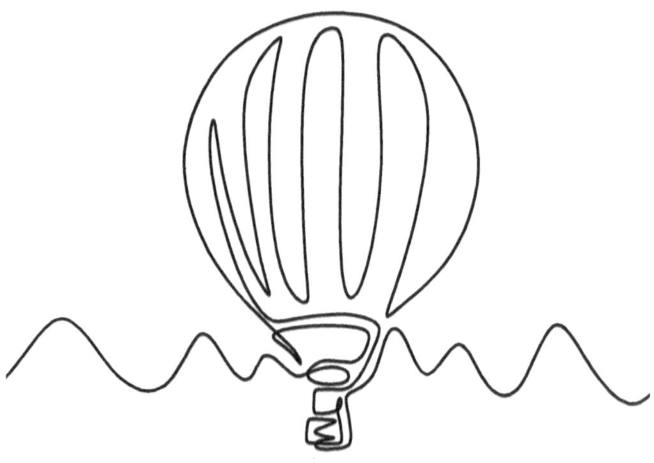

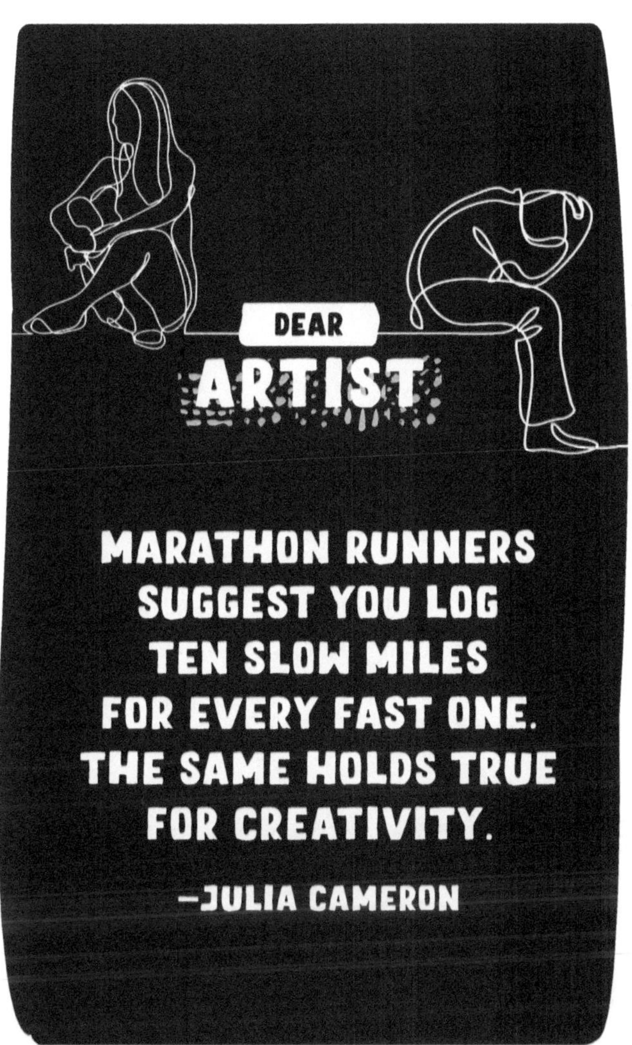
DEAR
ARTIST

MARATHON RUNNERS
SUGGEST YOU LOG
TEN SLOW MILES
FOR EVERY FAST ONE.
THE SAME HOLDS TRUE
FOR CREATIVITY.

—JULIA CAMERON

DEAR ARTIST,

Social media can be detrimental to the inner life of an artist.

It is touted as important, and while it can be used as a tool, scrolling through feeds that have been edited and curated to give off the impression of perfection and celebrity can do your soul more harm than good.

Stop looking to everyone else to inspire you. To help you get to the next step. Try to be more concerned with your inner steps than your outer. If it's true that our outer reality is a reflection of our inner life, then we should be doing all we can to give ourselves inner peace, inner joy, inner serenity. Only then will our outside reality transform into the life we so desperately desire.

Social media breeds chaos. If you are an artist seeking to authentically express the things of the soul, then spending your downtime scrolling through the endless pages of those who make themselves out to be greater than they are will only bring you down to their level.

Stop trying to keep up with those who cause your soul turmoil. Learn to identify them, and get yourself as far away from them as you can. All that those feeds, posts, and likes will do is beat down your sacred sense of curiosity and discourage you from following your soul's whisper of inspiration.

Give yourself the gift of logging off for a while.

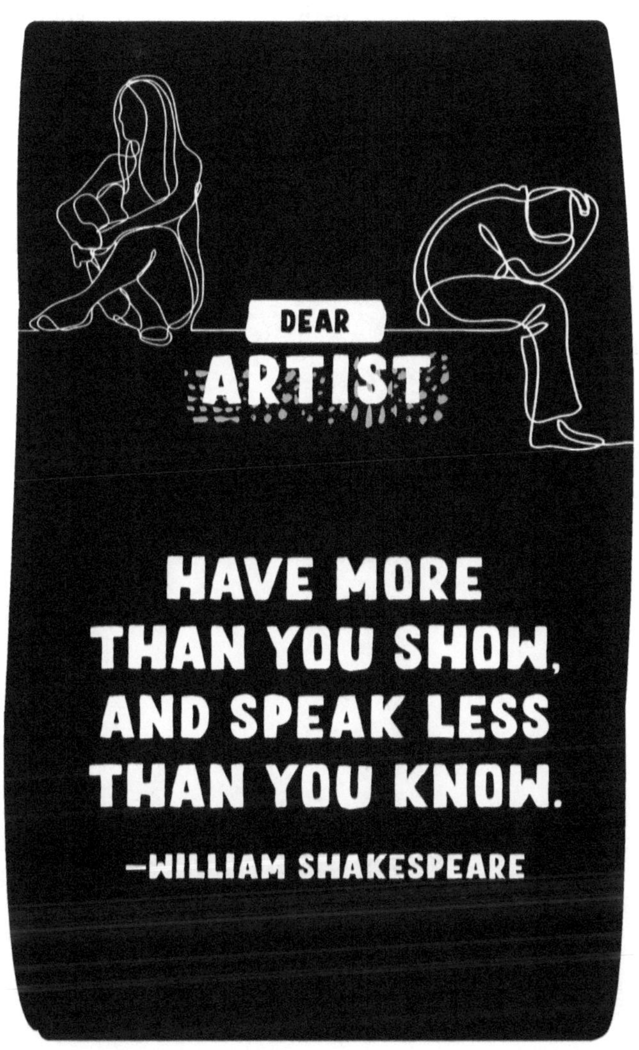

DEAR
ARTIST
HAVE MORE
THAN YOU SHOW,
AND SPEAK LESS
THAN YOU KNOW.
—WILLIAM SHAKESPEARE

DEAR ARTIST,

You did good today. Stop being so hard on yourself. Working every second doesn't bring the life of fulfillment you are searching for. Play just as hard as you work.

You did your very best today. Stop kicking yourself for not doing better. The unrealistic expectations you set for yourself only bring you misery. Look at everything you've accomplished and know that it is enough.

For today, you have done enough. More than enough.

And I am more proud of you than you could possibly believe.

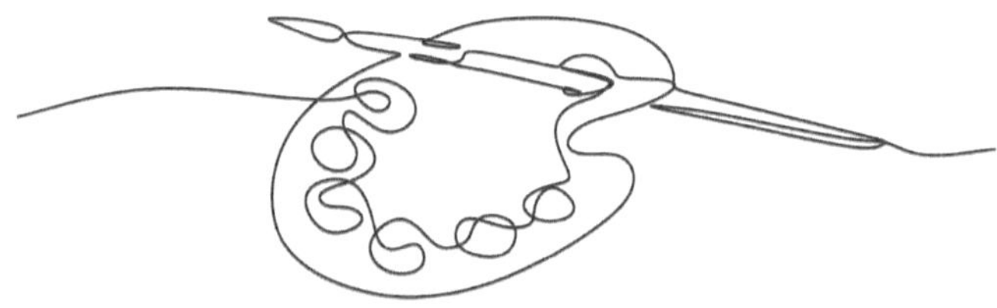

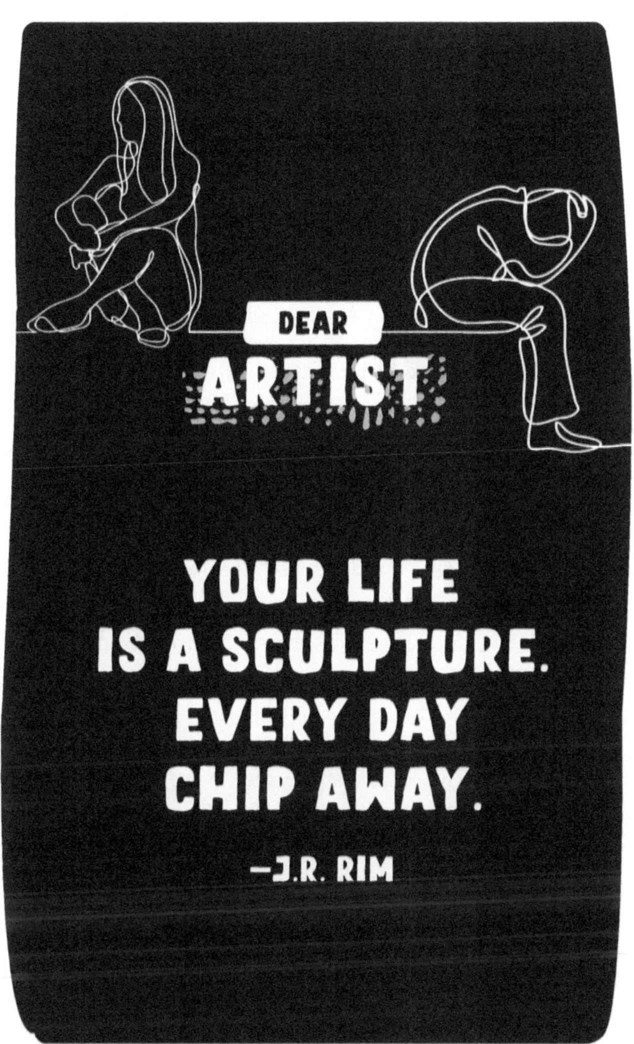
DEAR
ARTIST

YOUR LIFE
IS A SCULPTURE.
EVERY DAY
CHIP AWAY.

—J.R. RIM

DEAR ARTIST,

There are times when you wonder whether any of this will come to fruition. All the long hours, the money spent, the years gone by. People call this wasted time and in your heart of hearts, beneath all the armor you've built around yourself, you secretly wonder if their accusations may be true.

Allow me to let you in on a little secret I like to call The Echoes of The Universe. You see, an artist's life is like a three-way echo. Your desperate need to create is not just some pie in the sky fantasy born of your own devices. It was placed there from the beginning.

You were born with it.

The Universe has placed this call within you. Possibly since before you even knew what it was. When you awaken to the truth of the artistic desires within you and begin to take steps to see those desires realized, you have echoed back the Universe's call. And once you have done that, in the final stroke of this beautiful exchange, the Universe will affirm your echo with the success it had planned all along.

I cannot tell you when this success will take place. It may be tomorrow, it may be ten years from now.

But it will come. Have faith.

In the Universe's call and in the talent you have nurtured.

It will happen.

This is how the Universe works. Give yourself time.

And watch the tapestry of your life unfold.

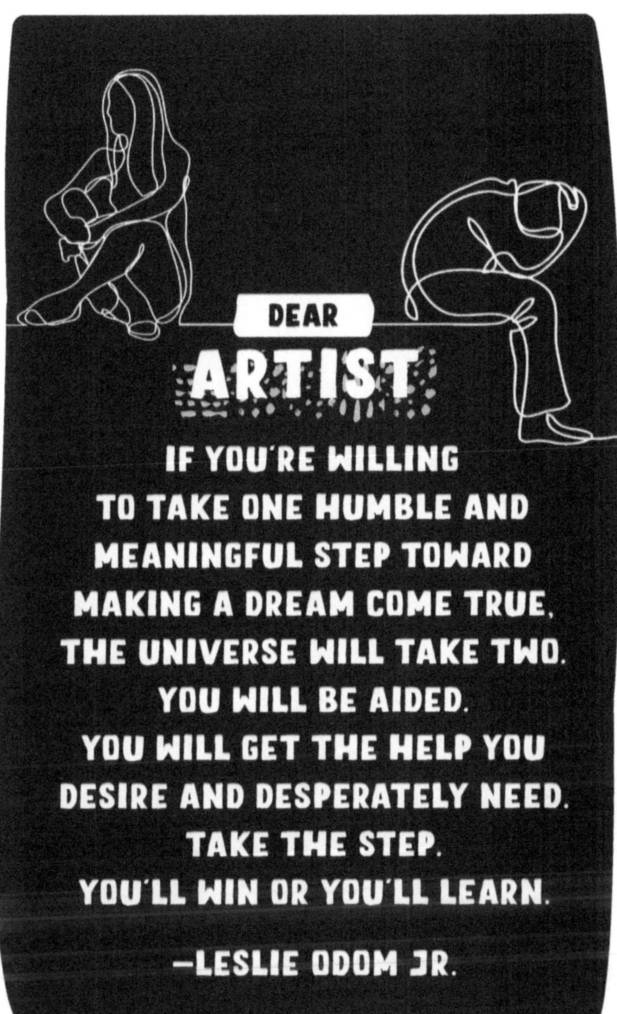
DEAR
ARTIST
IF YOU'RE WILLING
TO TAKE ONE HUMBLE AND
MEANINGFUL STEP TOWARD
MAKING A DREAM COME TRUE,
THE UNIVERSE WILL TAKE TWO.
YOU WILL BE AIDED.
YOU WILL GET THE HELP YOU
DESIRE AND DESPERATELY NEED.
TAKE THE STEP.
YOU'LL WIN OR YOU'LL LEARN.

—LESLIE ODOM JR.

DEAR ARTIST,

Those things that make your soul come alive—you *have* to do those things. Listen to me, these things are life. The essence of who we are. Learn to listen to what brings your soul life. Many of the voices you come across—including your own at times—will tell you those things are stupid and that you are wasting your time.

More often than not those voices are an indicator that you are on the right path.

Do what gives your soul life.

If you don't, what else is left?

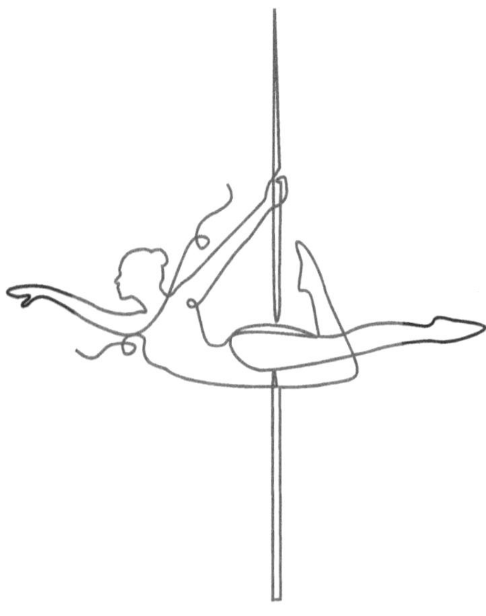

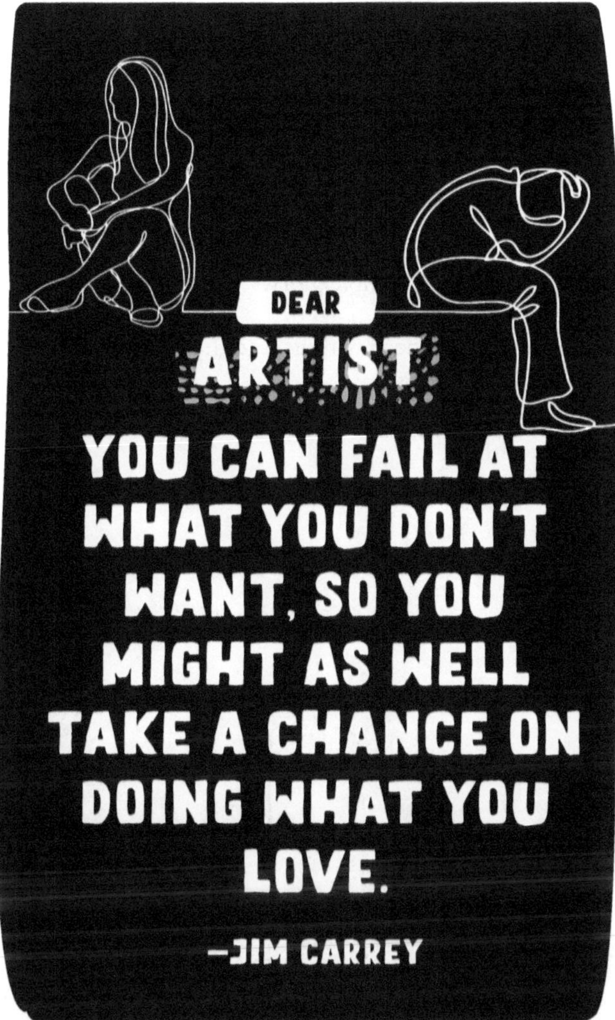
DEAR
ARTIST
YOU CAN FAIL AT WHAT YOU DON'T WANT, SO YOU MIGHT AS WELL TAKE A CHANCE ON DOING WHAT YOU LOVE.
—JIM CARREY

DEAR ARTIST,

Allow yourself to experience the full breadth of what it is to be human. False positivity robs you of coming face to face with your three dimensional, authentic self.

In fact, it does more harm than good. Shadow positivity is no positivity at all.

Feel what you are feeling. Don't try to stuff it away. Feel it in all it's passionate, terrible glory.

Take as long as you need with it. And then go on from there.

Each emotion is a unique piece of your puzzle. You wouldn't be whole without it.

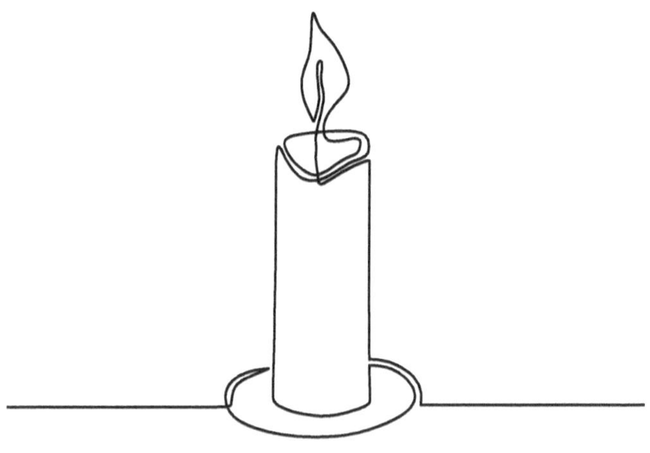

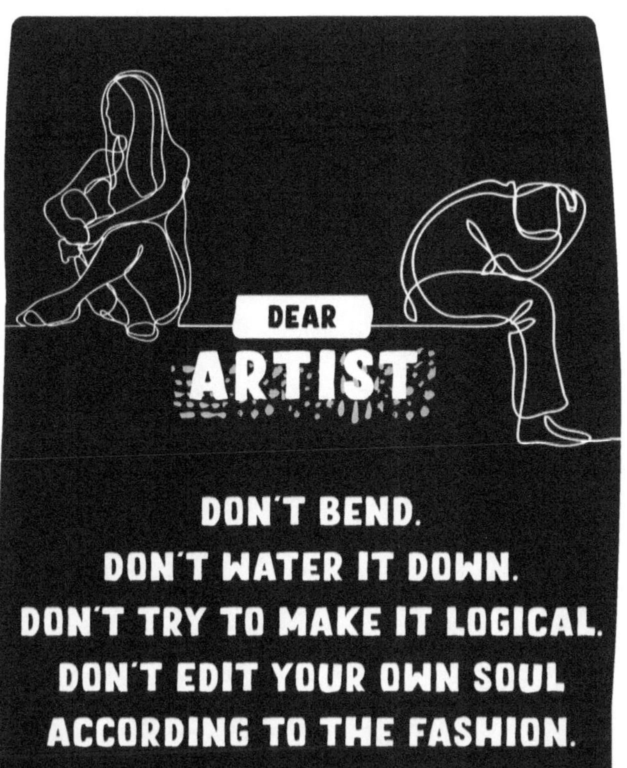

DEAR
ARTIST

DON'T BEND.
DON'T WATER IT DOWN.
DON'T TRY TO MAKE IT LOGICAL.
DON'T EDIT YOUR OWN SOUL
ACCORDING TO THE FASHION.
RATHER, FOLLOW YOUR MOST
INTENSE OBSESSIONS.

—ANNE RICE

DEAR ARTIST,

Take time to grieve. Be angry! Allow yourself the gift of being a fully formed human with robust, strong emotions. In the expression and follow-through of what you're feeling, you will find cleansing on the other side. Like a rainforest after a thunderstorm, your soul will be calm and washed anew.

And ready.

If not ready to move again yet, ready to wait.

Waiting is enough.

Wait for inspiration.

Wait for strength.

Wait for your soul to be ready and courageous once again.

It's okay. I'm proud of you.

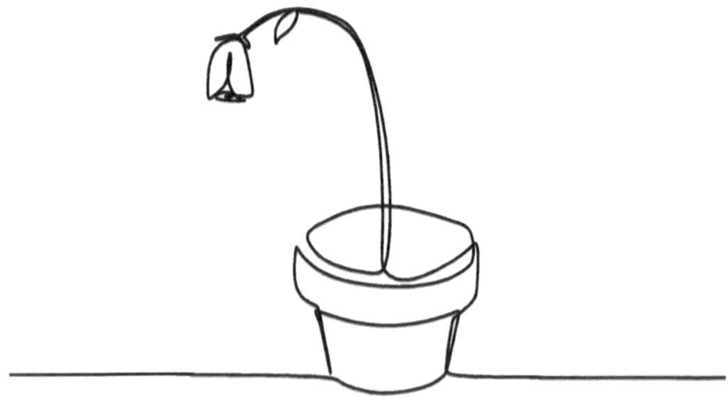

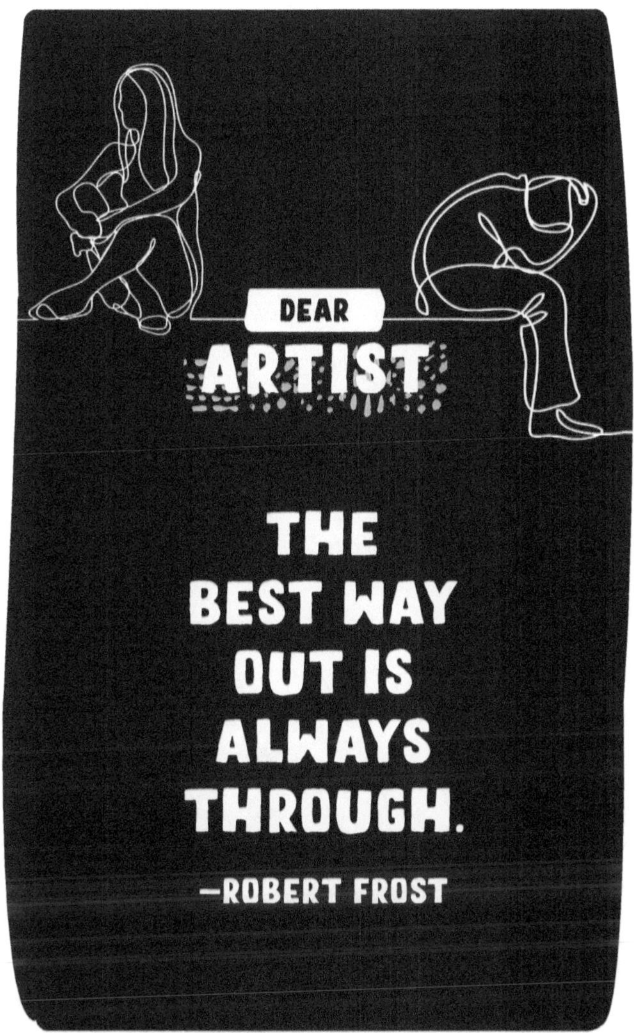
DEAR
ARTIST
THE
BEST WAY
OUT IS
ALWAYS
THROUGH.
—ROBERT FROST

DEAR ARTIST,

Tonight as I was painting, I realized something. At one point I messed up, got annoyed, and cursed under my breath at the misplaced colors drying on the page…

And then it struck me.

In that split second it hit me just how wrong that felt.

How wrong it was to criticize and feel bad about this "mistake." It is art! What is right? What is wrong? It is art.

There are no mistakes. I didn't mess up. And neither have you.

There is no right or wrong in art. There is just art.

Which is both immensely terrifying and incredibly freeing.

So create.

Be terrified.

And be free.

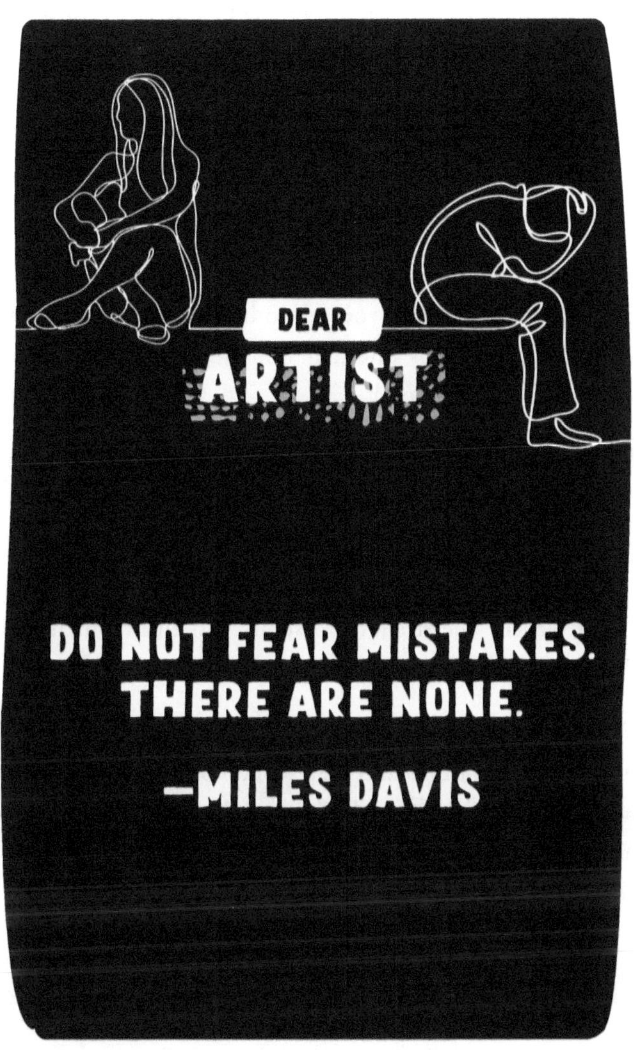
DEAR
ARTIST
DO NOT FEAR MISTAKES.
THERE ARE NONE.
—MILES DAVIS

DEAR ARTIST,

They say it's darkest just before dawn. But your world has been blacker than black for so long. You feel that everything is working against you. Every corner you turn only leads to a dead end. A missed opportunity. Another if-only. The bills are piling up and you feel that even one more shift at that soul-sucking job will put you over the edge.

It's okay to feel that way. None of this is your fault. And the circumstances you find yourself in have no bearing on your worth, as an artist or a human. You are seen. You are loved. And you are understood.

I know your world is crumbling. Your sanity is slipping away and you find yourself at the end of your rope.

Rock bottom. So this is what it feels like.

If you haven't the strength to stand, just turn your head a little bit. Look up.

For one moment remember who you were at the beginning. The bright eyes and the face full of hope. I'll bet that beginner would be proud of you right now, even in your misery. You've already come farther than you ever believed you could.

I can't tell you when it will end. But I can tell you that you've made it through every challenge you have ever faced.

Courage, my friend. Courage.

Just a little bit longer.

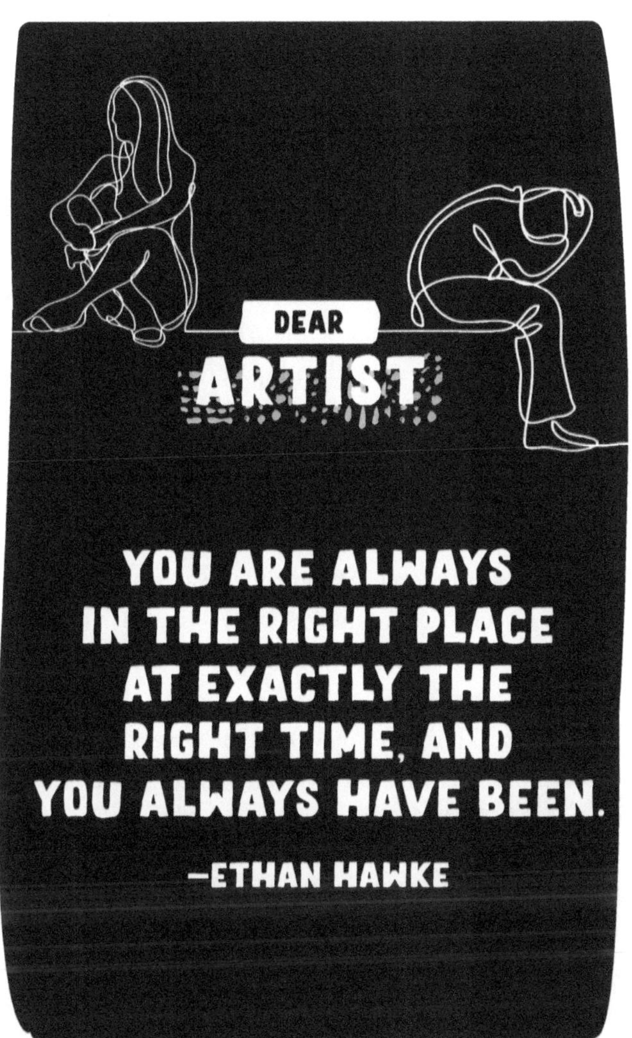
DEAR
ARTIST

YOU ARE ALWAYS
IN THE RIGHT PLACE
AT EXACTLY THE
RIGHT TIME, AND
YOU ALWAYS HAVE BEEN.

—ETHAN HAWKE

DEAR ARTIST,

So many of us are workaholics when it comes to our craft. "Artaholics," if you will. We feel that we must spend every second of every day working and creating. This could stem from any one of several sources, or a mixture of a few. It could be a desperate desire to have something work out so you are financially stable. It could be that you are trying to prove to a significant other, loved one, or yourself that you are actually good at what you do and that you are not wasting your life. It could be that you are using your art as a coping mechanism to deal with past trauma, and you fear that if you slow down, those memories and wounds will finally catch up to you.

But you cannot create without filling yourself up.

Meet interesting people. Spend time away from your desk. Go to museums. See a movie every once in a while. A novel can do wonders for the imagination. Nature is full of nurture. Visit that exotic restaurant that's always piqued your interest. Travel to a new city for a week just to soak in its atmosphere. This will not only enhance your creative endeavors, but will fulfill your personal life as well.

Live. Don't spend so much time trying to create a fulfilling life that you forget to actually live one.

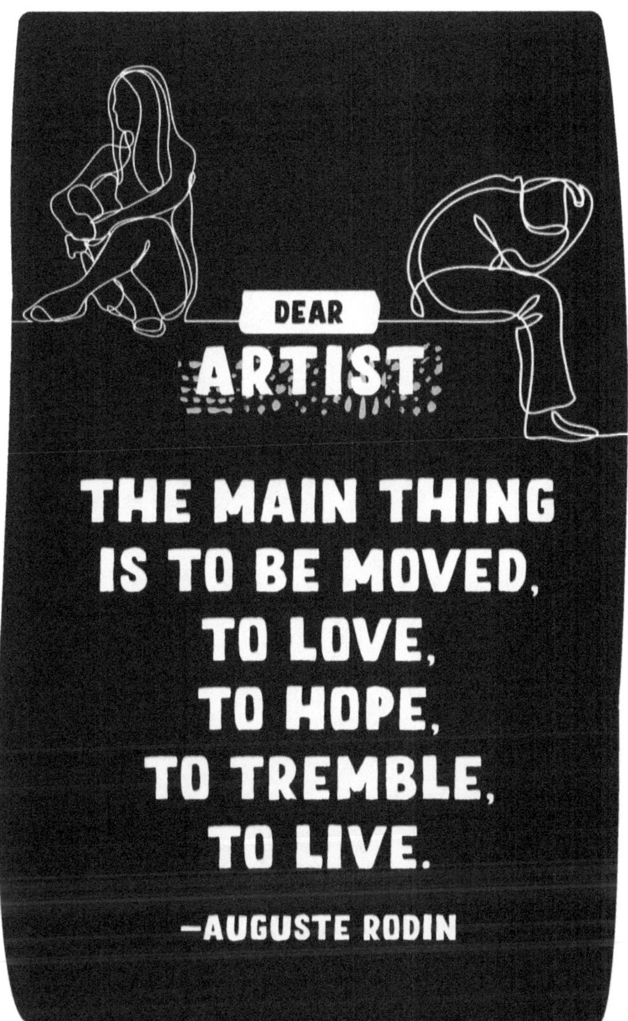
DEAR
ARTIST
THE MAIN THING
IS TO BE MOVED,
TO LOVE,
TO HOPE,
TO TREMBLE,
TO LIVE.
—AUGUSTE RODIN

DEAR ARTIST,

Progress, not perfection.

You are perfect in your progress.

You perfectionist. :)

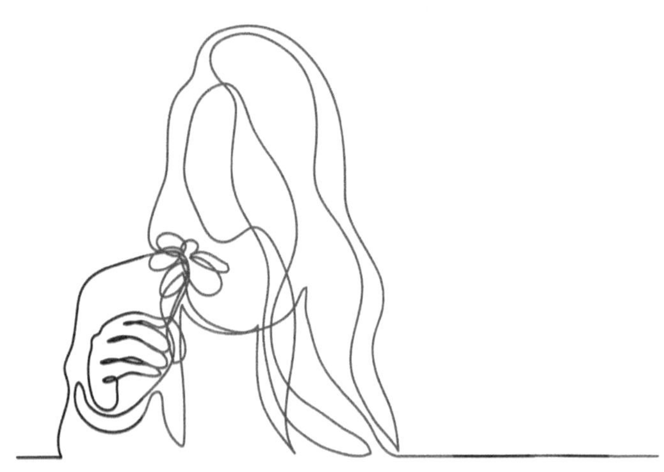

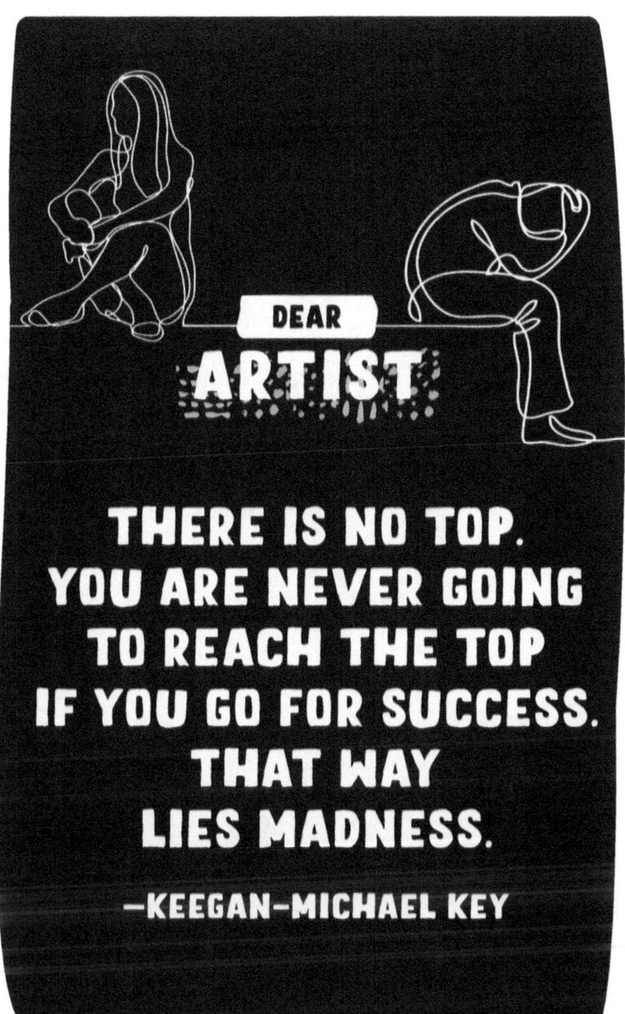
DEAR
ARTIST

THERE IS NO TOP.
YOU ARE NEVER GOING
TO REACH THE TOP
IF YOU GO FOR SUCCESS.
THAT WAY
LIES MADNESS.

—KEEGAN-MICHAEL KEY

DEAR ARTIST,

Remember to listen to that tiny voice inside you. Reassuring you. Reminding you that you will make it. *That* is the truth. The other voice might be louder. The other voice might be screaming. But that little voice always finds a way through. It is always there.

And deep, deep down, in your heart of hearts, you know that tiny voice is the one telling the truth.

Fear is natural. Anxiety will be there. That voice of self-doubt is going to scream like there's no tomorrow. Acknowledge it, and focus on that whisper of truth.

As tiny as it is, it's solid as a rock.

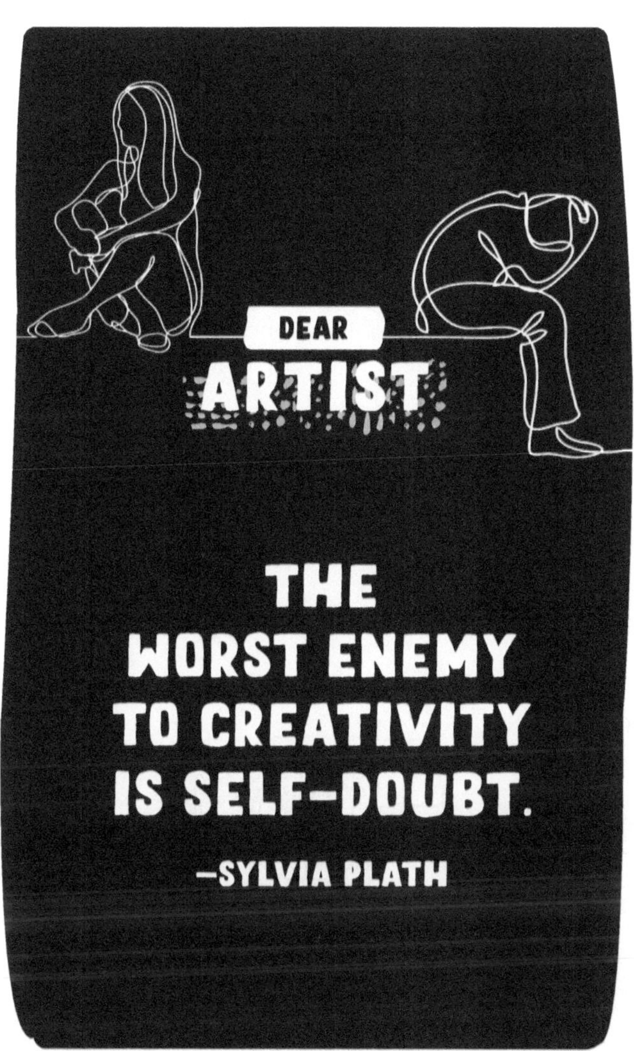

DEAR
ARTIST

THE
WORST ENEMY
TO CREATIVITY
IS SELF-DOUBT.
—SYLVIA PLATH

DEAR ARTIST,

All art is an attempt.

It is not for you to say whether your work is "good" or whether your work is "bad." It is your job to create.

The attempt is enough. You might surprise yourself, you might not. It doesn't matter. What does matter is that you respond to that little voice inside you, asking you to try.

Artists are Attempters. Join us in the ranks of the unknown.

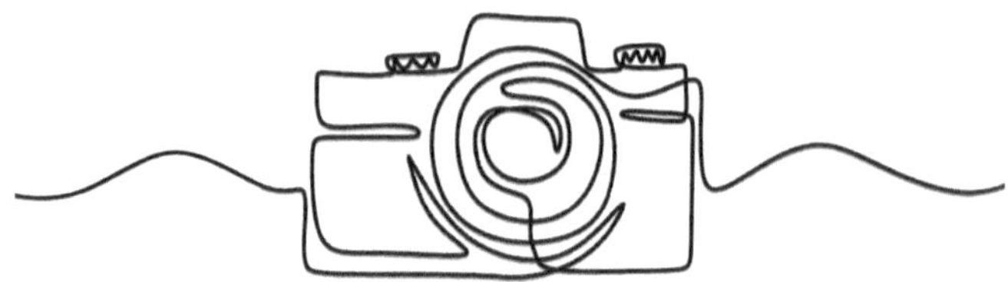

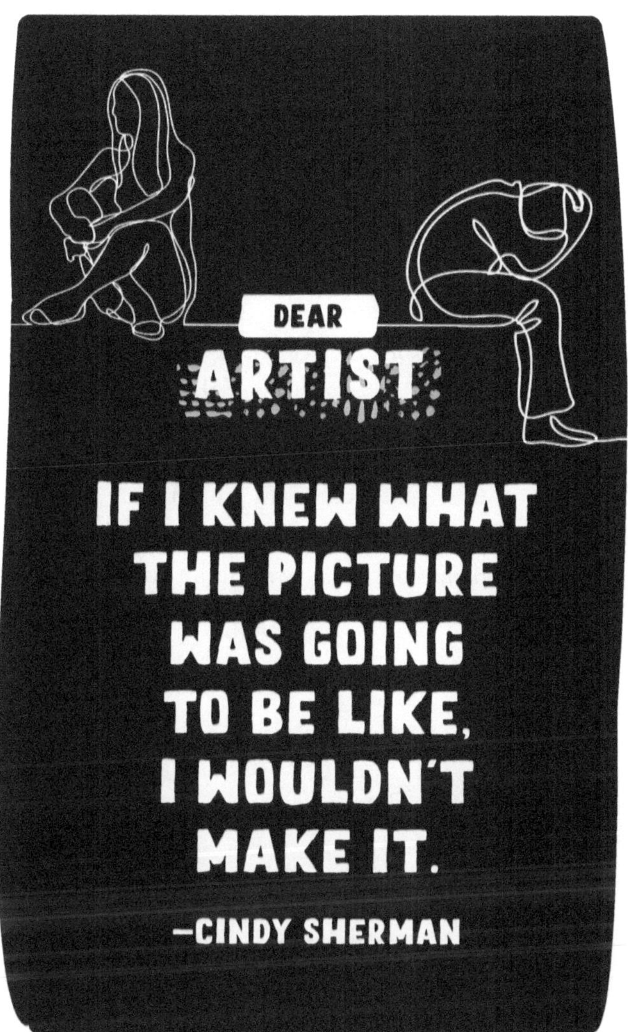

DEAR
ARTIST
IF I KNEW WHAT
THE PICTURE
WAS GOING
TO BE LIKE,
I WOULDN'T
MAKE IT.
—CINDY SHERMAN

DEAR ARTIST,

Most of us have heard that we are on average, a combination of the five people that we spend the most time with. This is equally true with art. We are all a product of the things we consume. The movies we watch, the books we read, the music we listen to, the podcasts we download, etc. Are you consuming wisely?

Consume great art. Even if it's not in your field. Go to the opera, even if you're a comedian. The sculptor's hands can learn a great deal from the ballerinas' grace. A day spent on a photographer's shoot can open the eyes of even the greatest writer.

Every bit of what you take in will inform your own work and make you more well rounded as a person. Open yourself up to elements of beauty you didn't even know were there to explore.

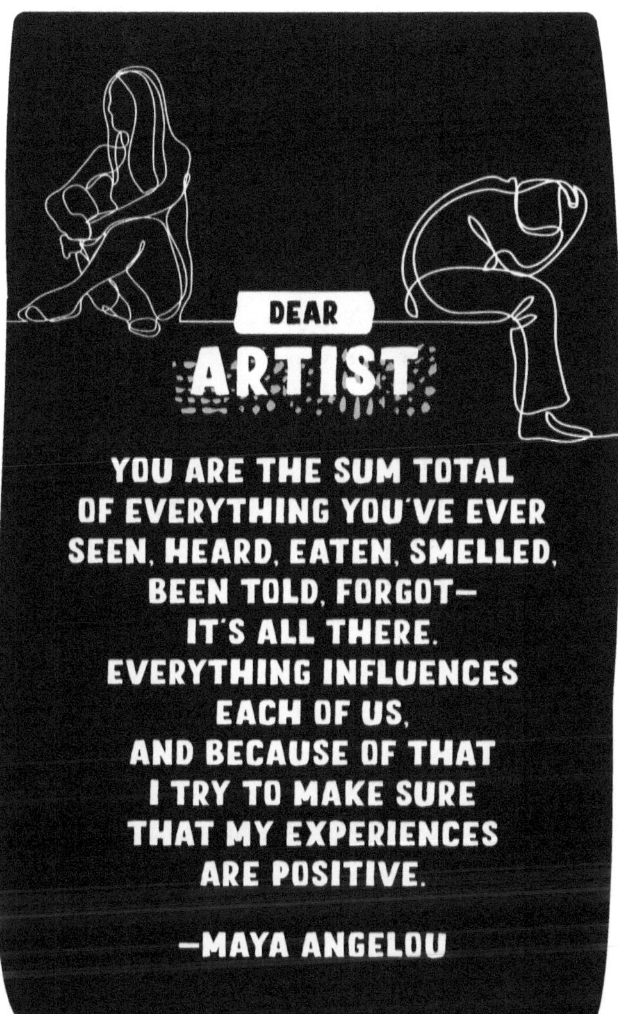

DEAR
ARTIST

YOU ARE THE SUM TOTAL
OF EVERYTHING YOU'VE EVER
SEEN, HEARD, EATEN, SMELLED,
BEEN TOLD, FORGOT—
IT'S ALL THERE.
EVERYTHING INFLUENCES
EACH OF US,
AND BECAUSE OF THAT
I TRY TO MAKE SURE
THAT MY EXPERIENCES
ARE POSITIVE.

—MAYA ANGELOU

DEAR ARTIST,

Rejection is something that we are all too familiar with. Half the time we invent and create knowing full well that our ideas and artistic projects will be turned down.

But continue we do. And continue we must.

The very fact that you are rejected so often should be the biggest reason you refuse to quit on yourself.

We hear it all the time. "No," you didn't book the audition. "No," we don't want your manuscript. "No," we have no use for your little poems and drawings.

We receive so many "Nos" on this long, hard road. Don't add your own voice to the chorus by saying it yourself before they even have a chance to. The day is coming when, instead of the usual no, you're going to get a yes.

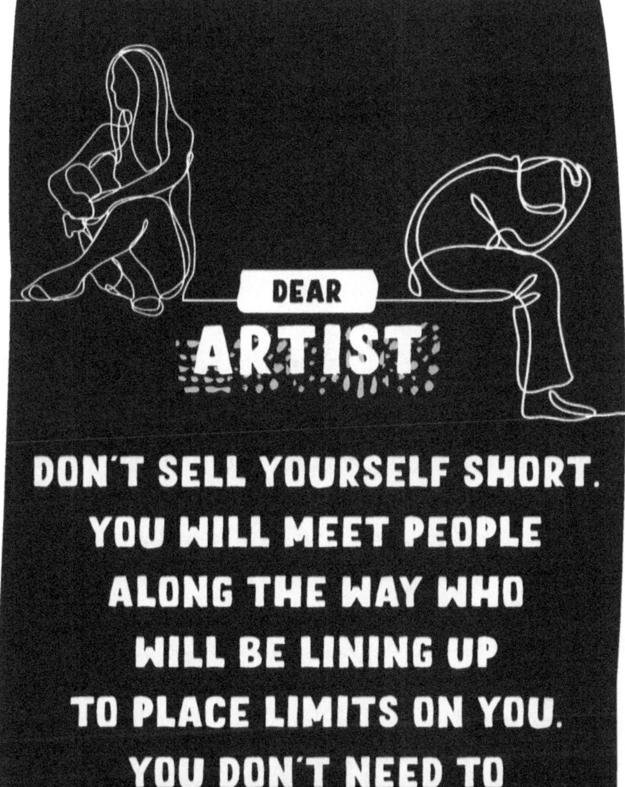

DON'T SELL YOURSELF SHORT.
YOU WILL MEET PEOPLE
ALONG THE WAY WHO
WILL BE LINING UP
TO PLACE LIMITS ON YOU.
YOU DON'T NEED TO
BEAT THEM TO THE PUNCH.

—LESLIE ODOM JR.

DEAR ARTIST,

I know life's got you down right now. I know you feel like you're in trouble. Sometimes it just doesn't feel like it's worth it, does it?

The not knowing, the struggles, the uncertainty, the "maybe this will work"—the pain of the need to create. The need to show the world the lens through which you see.

I know life is the worst, and you probably feel like you're giving up. Slowly. Day by day. As time ticks by you feel the pressure of the future close in. You know the feeling of having to stare your dream square in the face and insist that it keep on living one more day.

A dream isn't something you get once and have forever. A dream is something you renew every single day. Some days you wake up and it's all you can do to resuscitate that dream. Just to keep it alive for another twenty-four hours. Some weeks are like this, some months … some entire seasons are like this. Day in and day out, it takes all your strength just to bring your dream back from the brink. I know you're down and that famous "starving artist" lifestyle is rearing its head with all it's ugly might.

Not quite the Norman Rockwell painting we all thought it would be, huh?

For this season, stop looking at your dream as a whole. Stop looking at the finish line.

How am I going to get to the Oscars?
When will my shows sell out?
Will I ever write a bestselling novel?

You are not in charge of your legend. The result is not yours. Only the work. Do the work.

Does your soul dare to dream … today? Is the need within you … today?

Then dream today. Allow your soul to dream one more day. And then tomorrow … is the need still there? Then allow your soul to dream again.

A dream is a fire you rekindle every single day. And even if yours has slowly died down to an ember, it's still an ember. It's still glowing. It's still too hot for the human hand to touch. There is still life in your darkness.

You are an artist today.

Dream today.

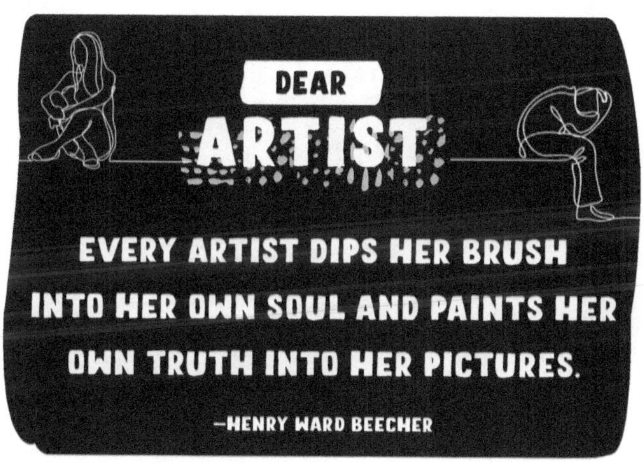

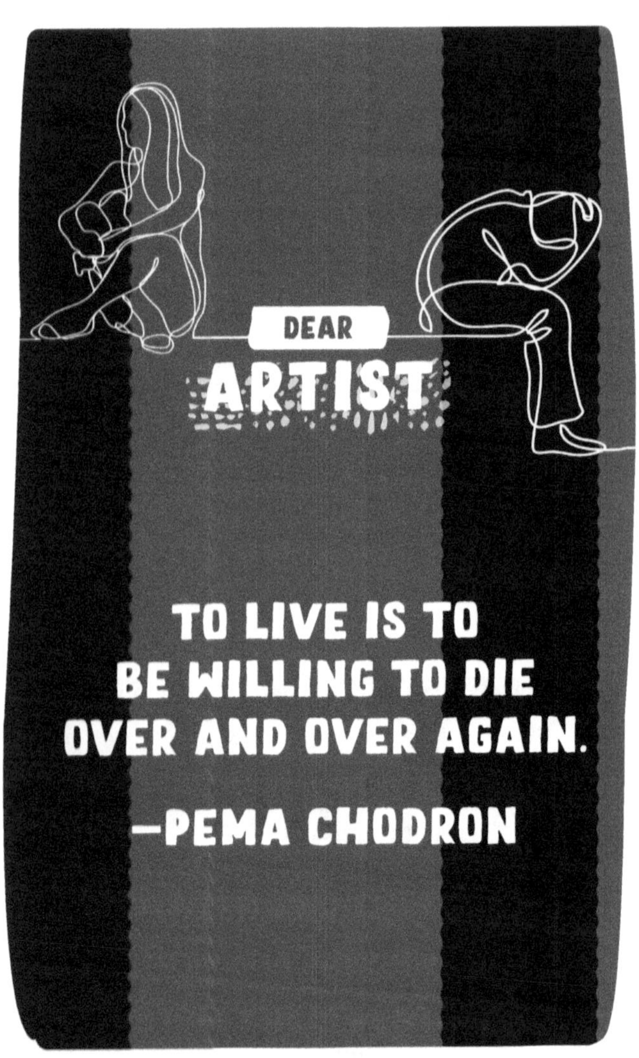

DEAR
ARTIST

TO LIVE IS TO
BE WILLING TO DIE
OVER AND OVER AGAIN.

—PEMA CHODRON

DEAR ARTIST,

In a previous letter I told you to wait for inspiration. That is absolutely true. But the flip side of that coin is that sometimes we wait too long. Our patient inaction turns into procrastination, or an excuse to put off something we know we need to do, but are too fearful to start. We end up no longer waiting out of trust and faith, but instead hold ourselves back in anxiety and self-doubt.

Sometimes you've gotta take the bull by the horns and just do the damn thing, even if you don't know exactly what that thing is yet. When your soul is fidgety and restless, it's time to look around and just start something. Anything.

Only you will know the difference between the need to wait and the need to move. And I believe, if you're honest with yourself, you already know what it is you need to do.

Now is the time for action. You'll find your footing as you start to climb.

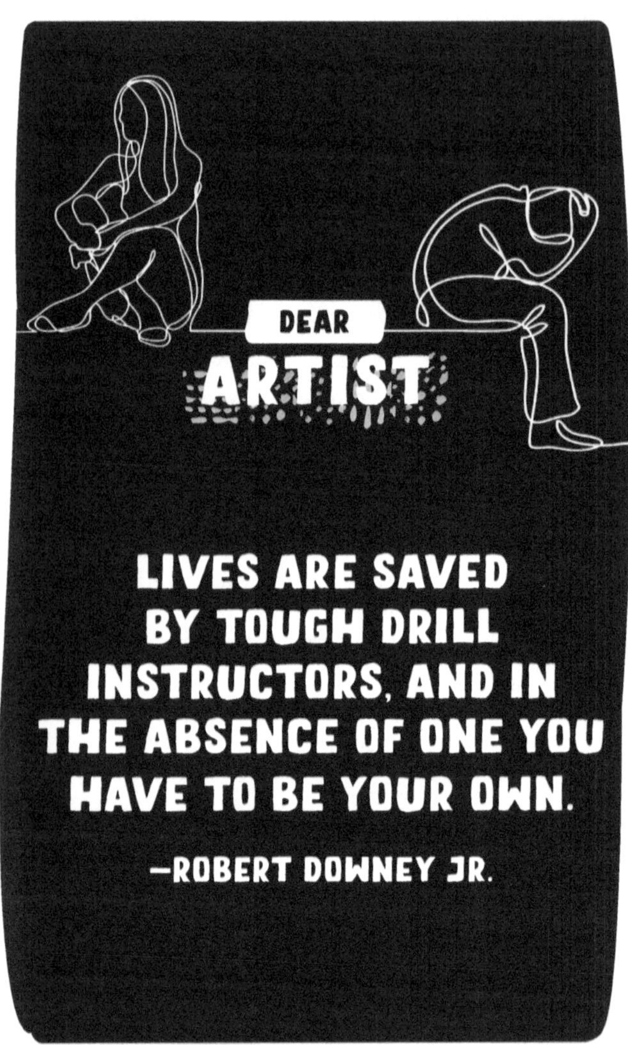

DEAR
ARTIST

LIVES ARE SAVED
BY TOUGH DRILL
INSTRUCTORS, AND IN
THE ABSENCE OF ONE YOU
HAVE TO BE YOUR OWN.

—ROBERT DOWNEY JR.

DEAR ARTIST,

Remember to keep going. Remember that just because it's hard doesn't mean you're on the wrong path. Remember that you're doing something incredibly brave. It's alright to turn around every once in a while and remind yourself just how far you've come.

Look at your steps. Look at your progress.

Here's to you, my friend. And here's to me. Here's to us.

And to the dream.

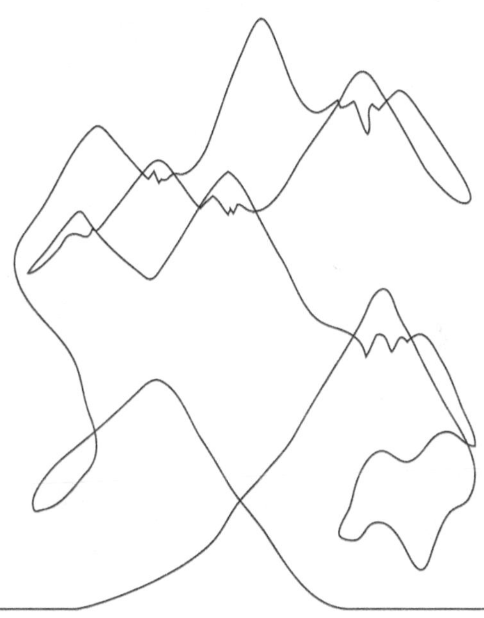

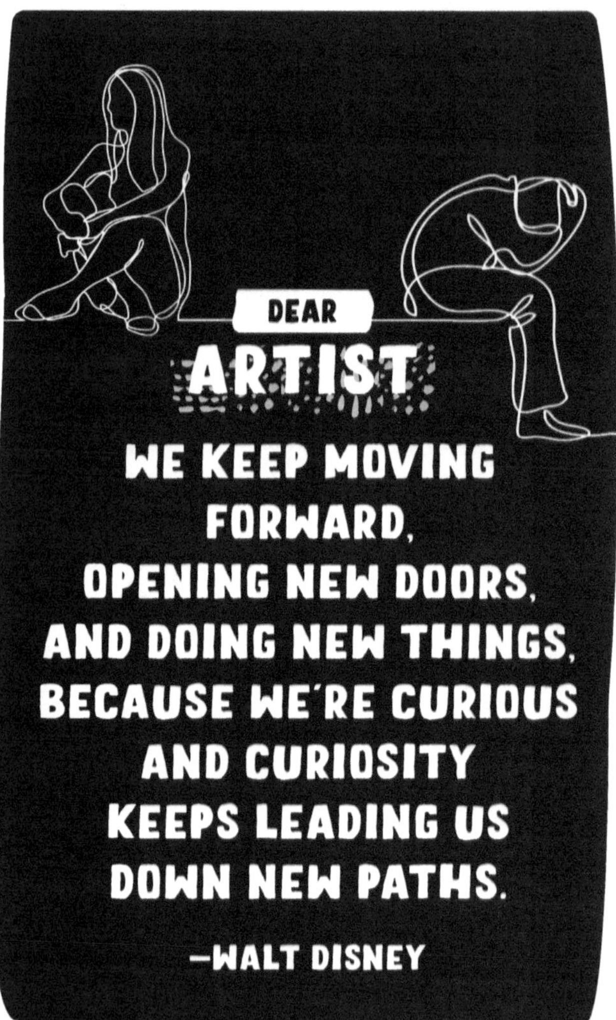
DEAR
ARTIST
WE KEEP MOVING
FORWARD,
OPENING NEW DOORS,
AND DOING NEW THINGS,
BECAUSE WE'RE CURIOUS
AND CURIOSITY
KEEPS LEADING US
DOWN NEW PATHS.
—WALT DISNEY

DEAR ARTIST,

You are going through the artist's birthing process. And yes, the labor pains are heavy. Heavier than you ever could have imagined. But sometimes being birthed feels just the same as being put to death. There is very little distinction between the two, and sometimes we don't know which one we are going through until some time has passed.

While there is so much uncertainty, so much you don't know, I can tell you one thing that is sure as the dawn; you will come out the other side of this. And when you do, you will be different. The creative birthing process never leaves anyone unchanged. And that change will make you more fully alive than ever before.

Some births have complications, and some are quick and easy. We don't get to choose how intense our process is. While this pain might be the worst thing you have ever felt, soon you will be able to breathe fresh air. You will be able to see bright colors. The fog will lift and the path before you will shine out ever clearer.

Embrace your rebirth.

Welcome the labor pains that you've so long been fighting.

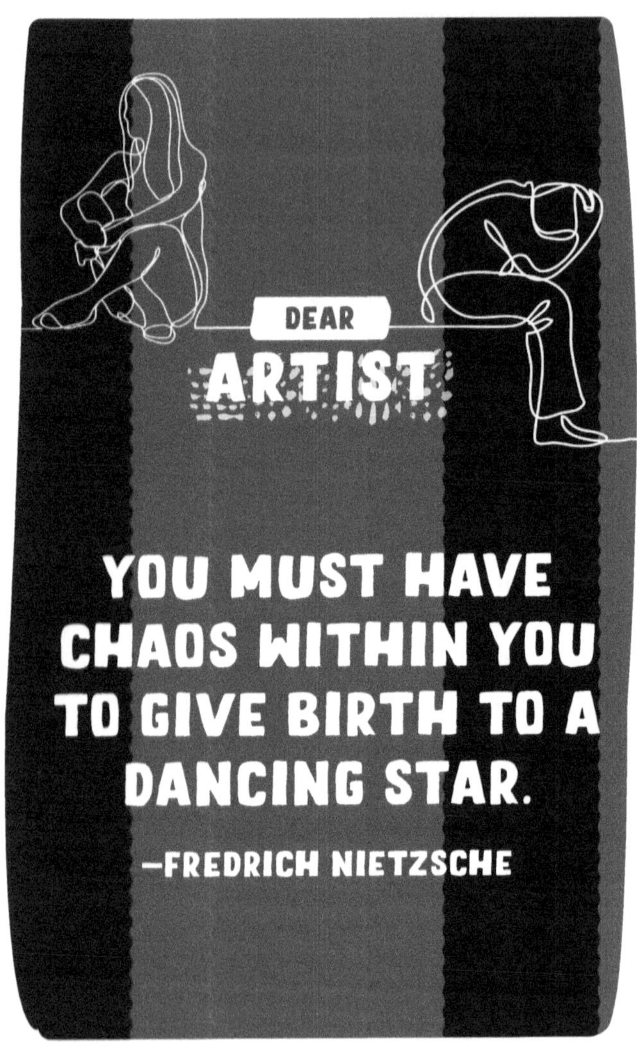
DEAR
ARTIST

YOU MUST HAVE
CHAOS WITHIN YOU
TO GIVE BIRTH TO A
DANCING STAR.

—FREDRICH NIETZSCHE

DEAR ARTIST,

If you have the opportunity to give a new artist a shot, do it.

See them as a younger version of yourself. Tell them the things that you needed to hear when you were at that stage. We all started somewhere and we all started with someone willing to take a chance on us. Brand new doesn't have to mean bad, it can just mean inexperienced. If you can give someone the opportunity to grow—and grow well—you will be giving them the greatest gift that is in your power to give.

This isn't about competition. We are all in this crazy artistic life together. As one.

Always be looking for opportunities to give back and pass along your wisdom.

Be the mentor that you needed, even if it's only for a short season.

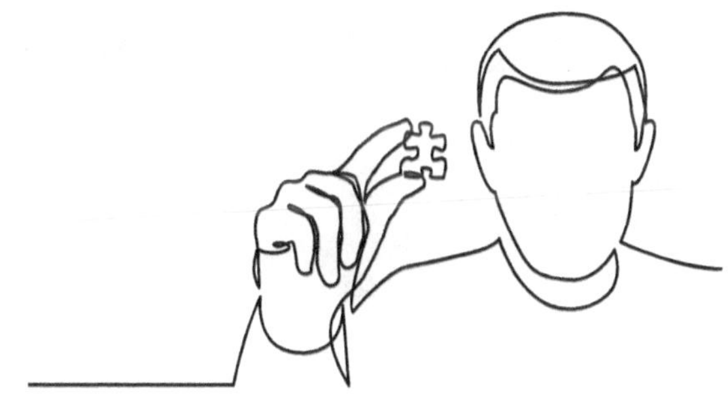

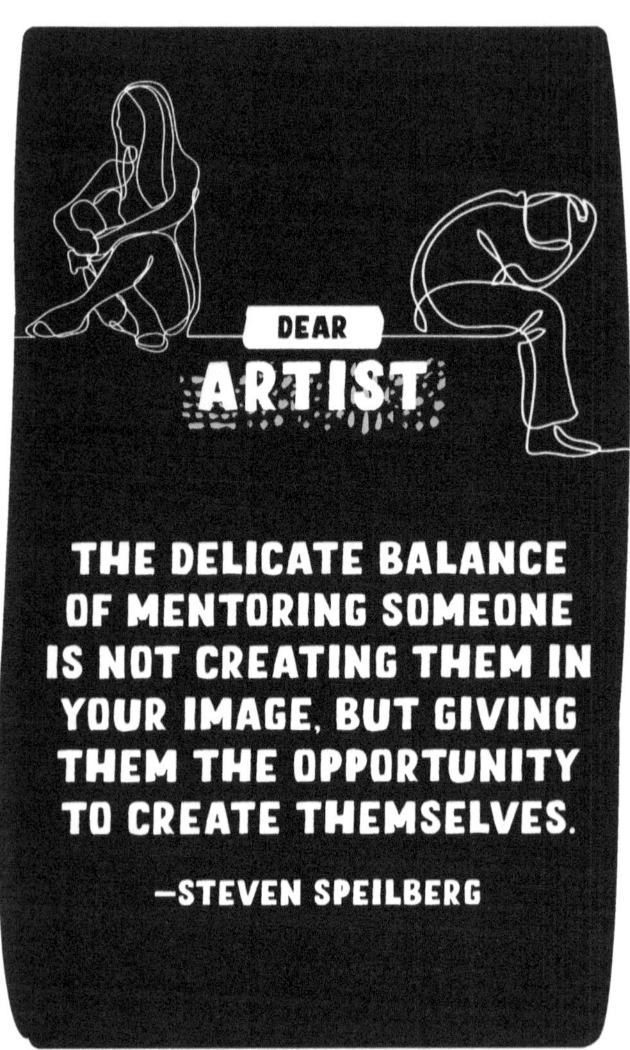

DEAR
ARTIST
THE DELICATE BALANCE OF MENTORING SOMEONE IS NOT CREATING THEM IN YOUR IMAGE, BUT GIVING THEM THE OPPORTUNITY TO CREATE THEMSELVES.
—STEVEN SPEILBERG

DEAR ARTIST,

Celebrate the small victories just as readily as you do the big ones.

Sometimes our eyes are so fixated on our huge and grandiose goals that we run right past all the tiny markers that are placed in our path, cheering us on along the way. It's easy to look past these as unimportant, especially if we lack self-worth, but what a mistake that would be. You are just as worthy of celebration in your quiet moments alone as you are on stage receiving that award. Maybe even more so.

You got a callback, but didn't get the part? Celebrate. You wrote a paragraph of that story that's been playing on your mind? Celebrate. Your short film made it into a local festival, but was rejected by Cannes? Celebrate. You finally figured out how to transition that chord? Celebrate. You danced your way through an entire song with only one mistake? Celebrate.

The steep, rough mountain of your dream is scaled by the thousand tiny steps it takes to get there. Your last step to victory is no more important than your first. Look for these small steps. Often they don't jump out at you, but they are there nonetheless. Silently watching with love and willing you to keep going just a little bit farther.

Live in the moment. Keep your eyes open. And celebrate the small victories.

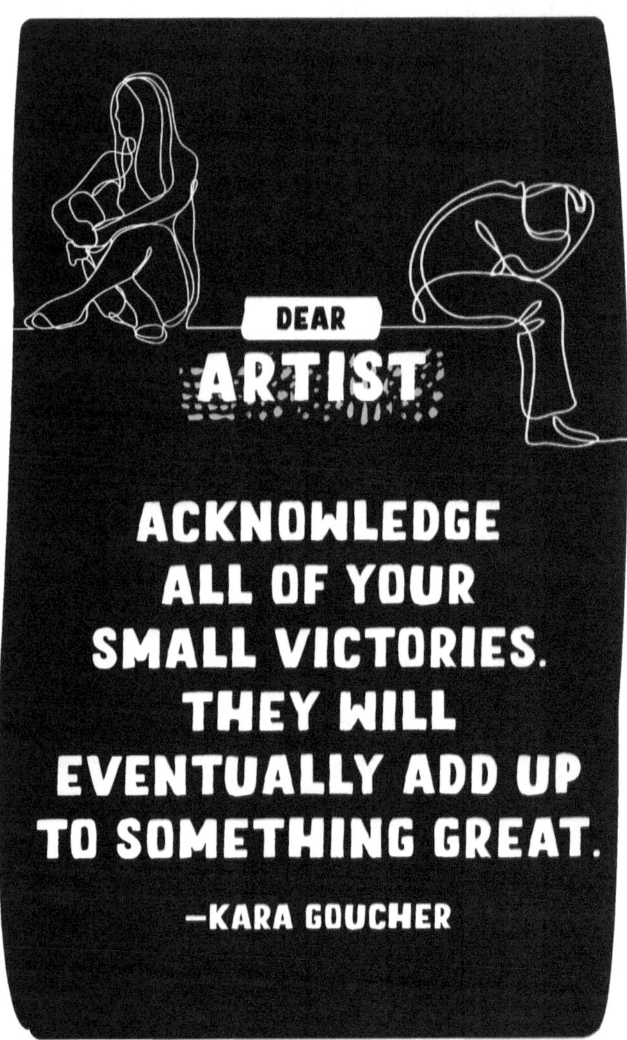

DEAR
ARTIST
ACKNOWLEDGE ALL OF YOUR SMALL VICTORIES. THEY WILL EVENTUALLY ADD UP TO SOMETHING GREAT.
—KARA GOUCHER

DEAR ARTIST,

Don't have a backup plan.

If you do, you will use it.

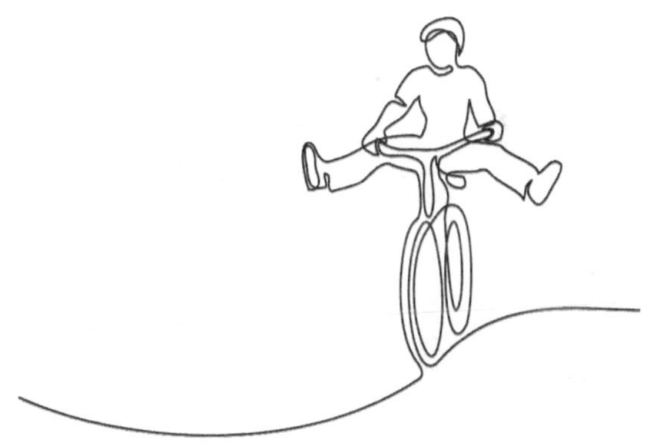

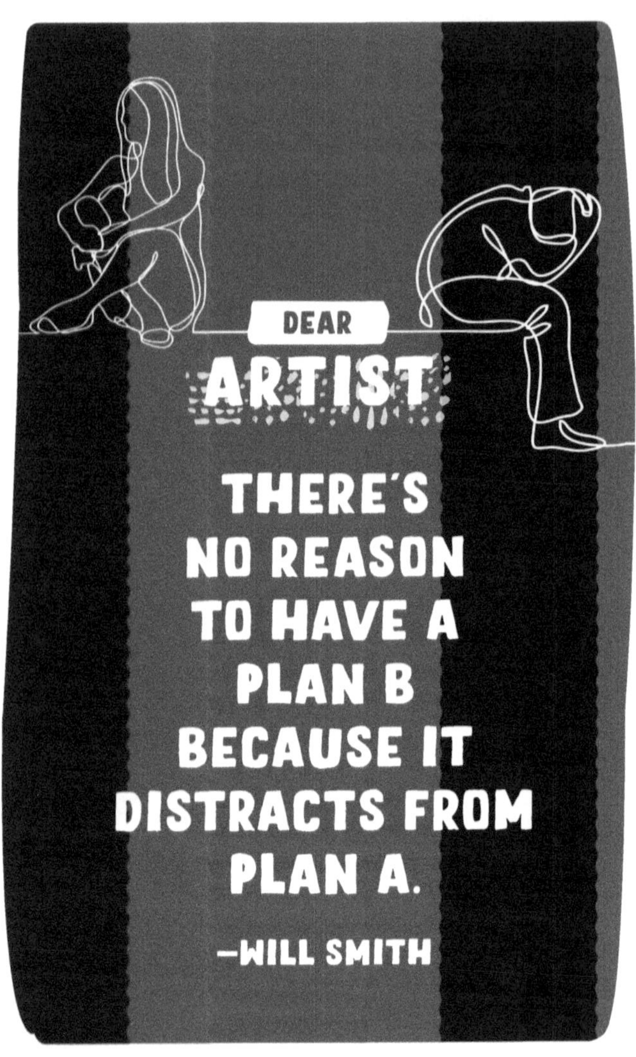
DEAR
ARTIST

THERE'S
NO REASON
TO HAVE A
PLAN B
BECAUSE IT
DISTRACTS FROM
PLAN A.

—WILL SMITH

DEAR ARTIST,

It is proven to be true that when everything else is stripped of the human race, when we are scared and uncertain and it feels like the end is near, we are in need of three things.

1. The Necessities for Life.
2. Community
3. Art

Art is a noble pursuit. Inextricably woven into the fabric of life. When everything else crumbles around us, humans long for and search for art to help us make sense of a naturally chaotic world. Remember that when your wires get crossed and things get muddled.

Art is a noble pursuit.

Hold your head high, and proudly pursue it.

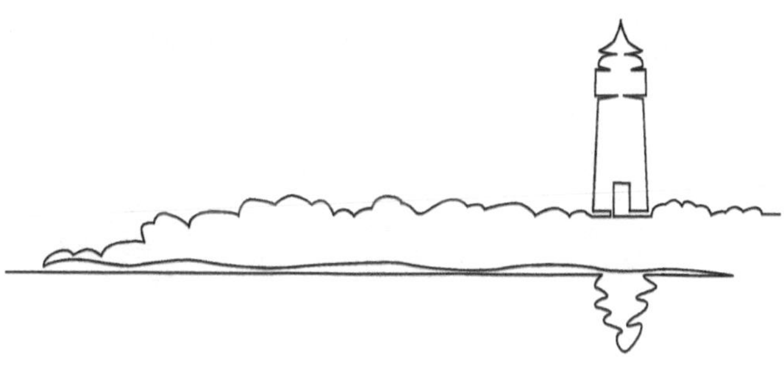

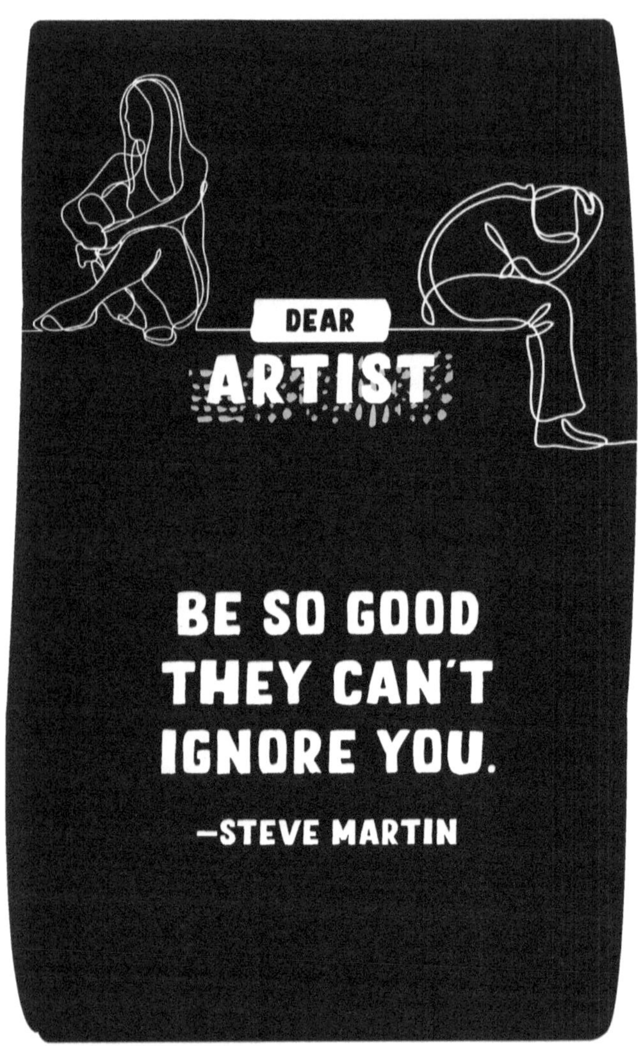

DEAR
ARTIST

BE SO GOOD
THEY CAN'T
IGNORE YOU.
—STEVE MARTIN

DEAR ARTIST,

Originality is not about saying something that has never been said, nor is it about doing something that has never been done. It is not achieved through long hard nights laboring in thought, practice, and sweat.

Originality is about perspective. You already have it.

To you the idea you have may seem obvious, or appear like nothing special. Because you live in your own head all day every day, the thoughts that come in and go out rarely appear unique. But they are. Despite what your inner critic may tell you, they are. They only seem ordinary to you because you're the one thinking them.

Your perspective is unique to you and if you are allowing yourself to honestly create from that one of a kind perspective, your art will be as singular and original as you are.

If you have a perspective, you have originality. Lean into it.

Unapologetically embrace your originality by unapologetically embracing yourself.

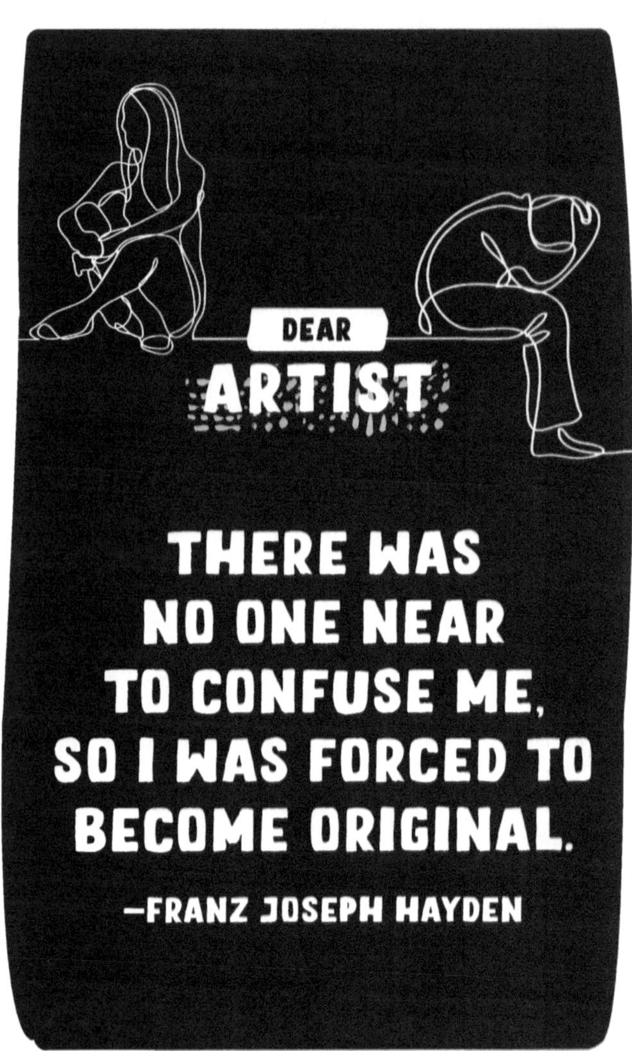

DEAR
ARTIST
THERE WAS
NO ONE NEAR
TO CONFUSE ME,
SO I WAS FORCED TO
BECOME ORIGINAL.
-FRANZ JOSEPH HAYDEN

DEAR ARTIST,

Those times when you feel so deeply, when you believe you're going to burst from the sheer intensity of emotion ... Those are creative growing pains. You're becoming bigger. Developing size as an artist. Those are emotional and artistic growing pains. Welcome them.

Let them flow through you. Feel them as deeply as possible.

Allow yourself to expand. Don't try to lessen the pain, push it down, or deny it simply because it is uncomfortable.

Uncomfortable means it's working.

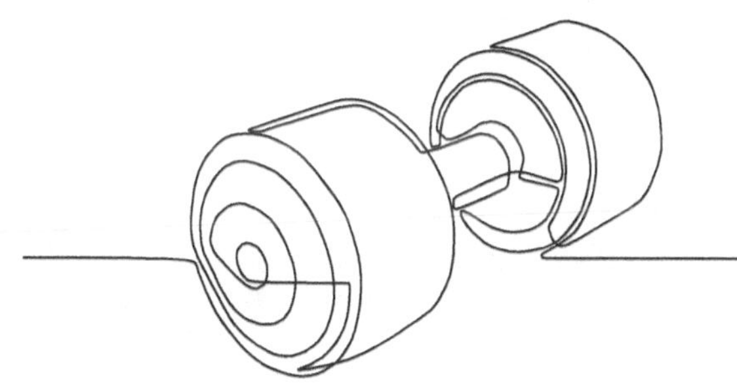

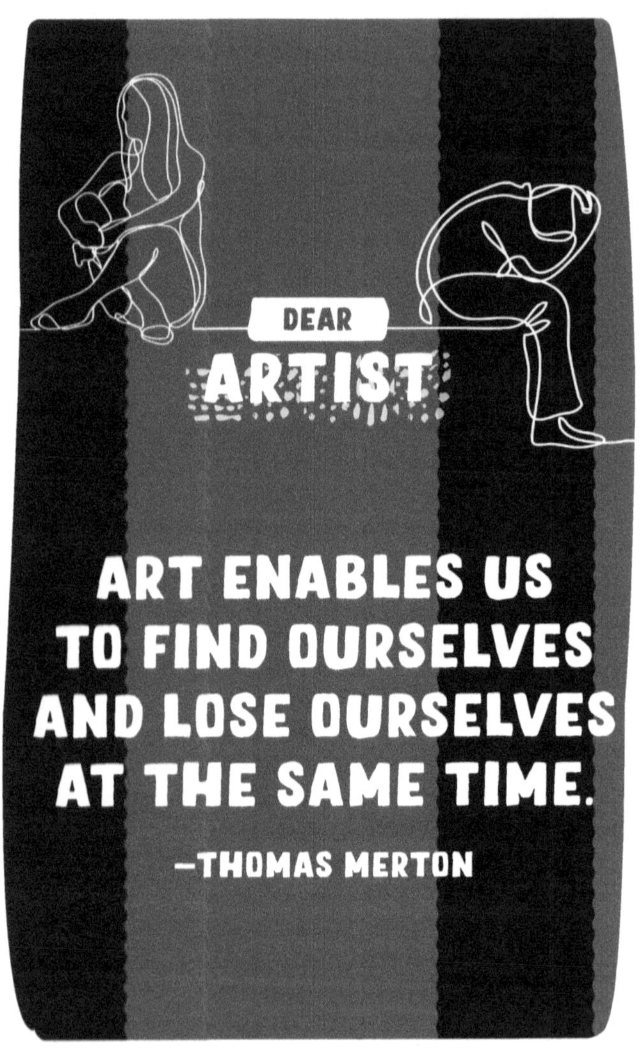
DEAR
ARTIST

ART ENABLES US
TO FIND OURSELVES
AND LOSE OURSELVES
AT THE SAME TIME.
—THOMAS MERTON

DEAR ARTIST,

No one gets to live, or have a say in your life but you.

They don't have that power, even if they believe they do.

You and only you are at the helm of your own ship.

Where you going, Captain?

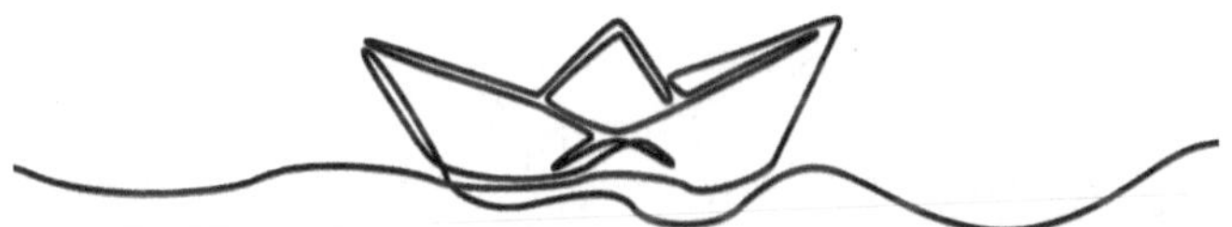

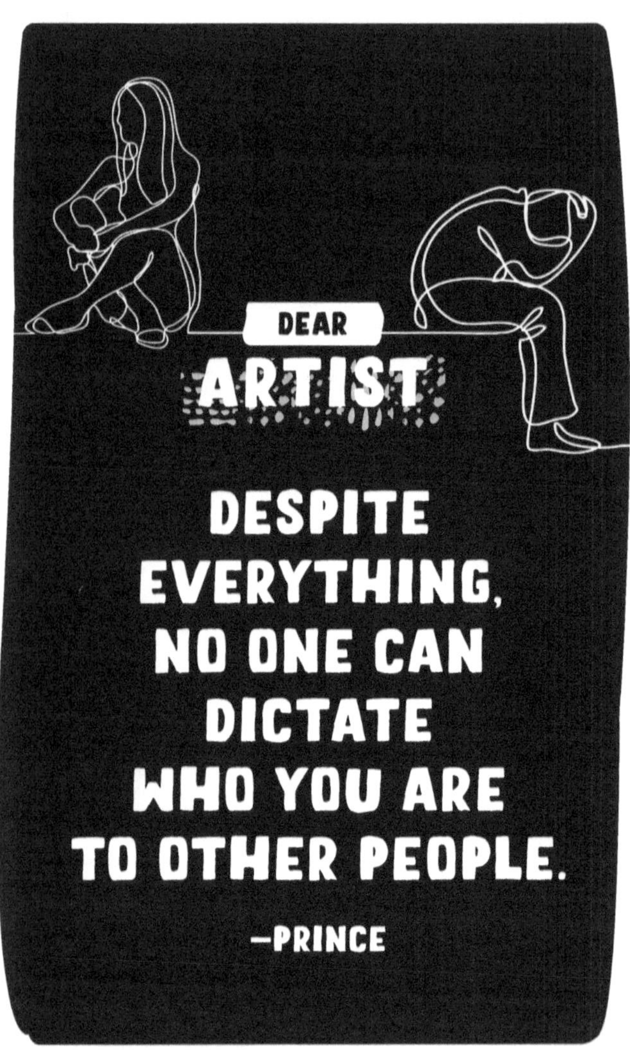
DEAR
ARTIST

DESPITE
EVERYTHING,
NO ONE CAN
DICTATE
WHO YOU ARE
TO OTHER PEOPLE.

—PRINCE

DEAR ARTIST,

You are in a season that may or may not be familiar. A season of downtime. This may strike panic into your soul, as it often does mine, but what if we looked at it from another perspective.

Just because the phone isn't ringing and emails aren't coming in doesn't mean you have become irrelevant, or that no one believes in you anymore, or they have finally figured out you're a fraud.

This could be the Universe's way of telling you to slow down. A sacred time of reconnection … to yourself.

Take this time to look inward. Are there areas of life that have fallen into disrepair? Healing that is long overdue? That still small voice inside you that is always pointing out the next step (but nothing more) knows when it is time to pause and reconnect to yourself.

If you are going to be productive, then you must take time to rest. If not, you will simply spin your wheels in a panic, wondering why you're not going anywhere.

You have permission to rest. And in resting, you will be the most productive that you have possibly ever been.

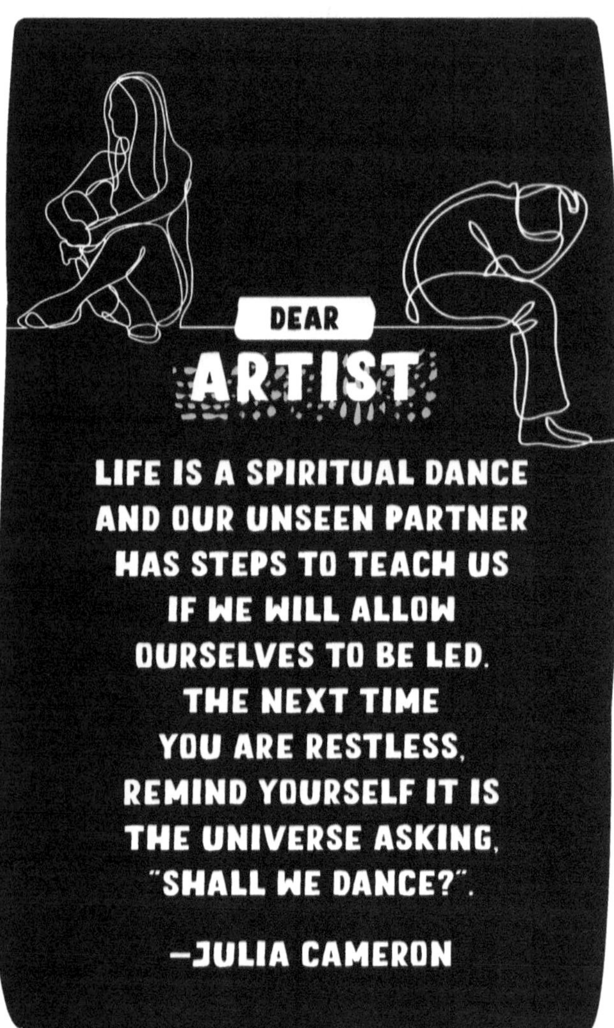

DEAR
ARTIST

LIFE IS A SPIRITUAL DANCE
AND OUR UNSEEN PARTNER
HAS STEPS TO TEACH US
IF WE WILL ALLOW
OURSELVES TO BE LED.
THE NEXT TIME
YOU ARE RESTLESS,
REMIND YOURSELF IT IS
THE UNIVERSE ASKING,
"SHALL WE DANCE?".

-JULIA CAMERON

DEAR ARTIST,

Step outside of yourself for a moment and objectively look at where you've come from. How far along the path you are. You've truly accomplished some amazing things. Just like at times it's hard to see the forest for the trees, sometimes it's hard to see your journey as a whole for the mud slogged steps you have been focused on for so long.

You've really come a long way. Did you ever think you'd be here? With this experience? Doing and pursuing the things you are now? Stop for a minute and take a good look at all the miles that have taken you to this point in your artistic expedition. Be proud of yourself! Take a moment to acknowledge your incredible achievements.

And all the things you've done so far? Even they pale in comparison to what's coming next.

Soak it all in. You don't have to be on the defense anymore.

Remain excited, expectant, open, and ready.

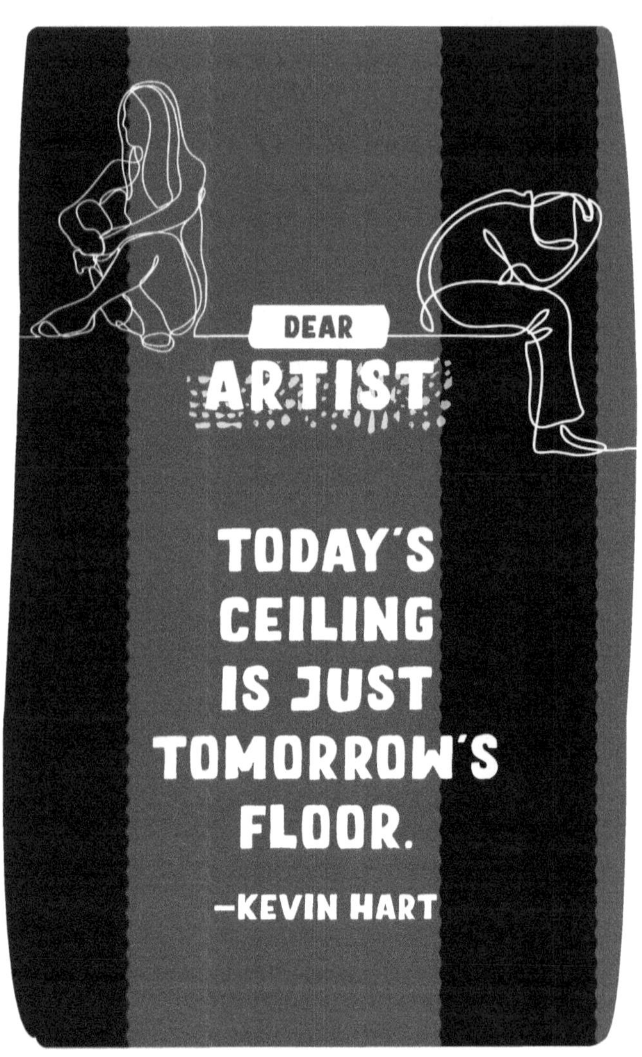

DEAR
ARTIST:

TODAY'S
CEILING
IS JUST
TOMORROW'S
FLOOR.
—KEVIN HART

DEAR ARTIST,

While art is inherently childlike—full of curiosity, play, and discovery—it also demands to be taken seriously. There is a weight to it that cannot be overlooked.

Michelangelo didn't become Michelangelo by seeing his work as a hobby. And Speilberg didn't become Speilberg by only filming when it was convenient. They became masters by throwing everything they had into their craft, holding nothing back.

How seriously are you willing to take your art? There is no instant gratification in the life of an artist. Stop looking for it. More than likely it will be a very long road, and cost you more than you ever imagined. But if this is something that is in your very blood, that you can see no life for yourself outside of, then it is worth it.

Because as agonizing a life as it is, the rewards that it yields are of equal, if not even greater value.

If this doesn't feel true for you right now, I want you to know that what you are feeling is valid. Don't let anyone downplay or undermine the trials and struggles that cut through to your core like a knife. I only ask that you have patience. As hard as it is to believe sometimes, every valley has a mountain. Every coin has two sides.

Oftentimes luck looks like hard work and dedication. Are you in this for the long haul, or are you not?

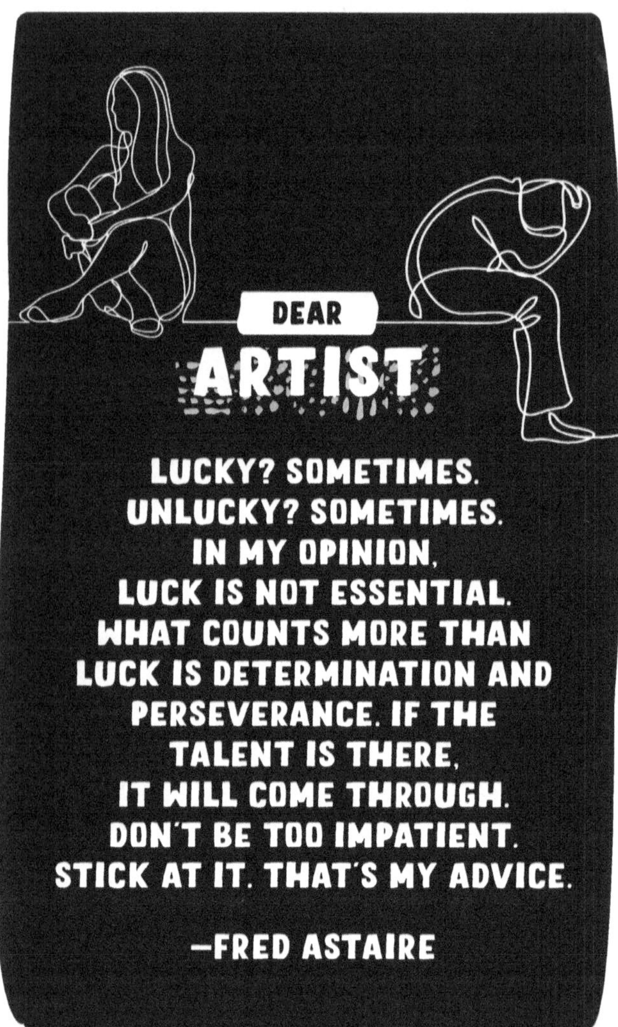

DEAR
ARTIST

LUCKY? SOMETIMES.
UNLUCKY? SOMETIMES.
IN MY OPINION,
LUCK IS NOT ESSENTIAL.
WHAT COUNTS MORE THAN
LUCK IS DETERMINATION AND
PERSEVERANCE. IF THE
TALENT IS THERE,
IT WILL COME THROUGH.
DON'T BE TOO IMPATIENT.
STICK AT IT. THAT'S MY ADVICE.

—FRED ASTAIRE

DEAR ARTIST,

If you find yourself at the end of your rope, desperately crying out to whatever powers that be because you cannot go one more day the way you've been going...

Take heart.

The process has already begun.

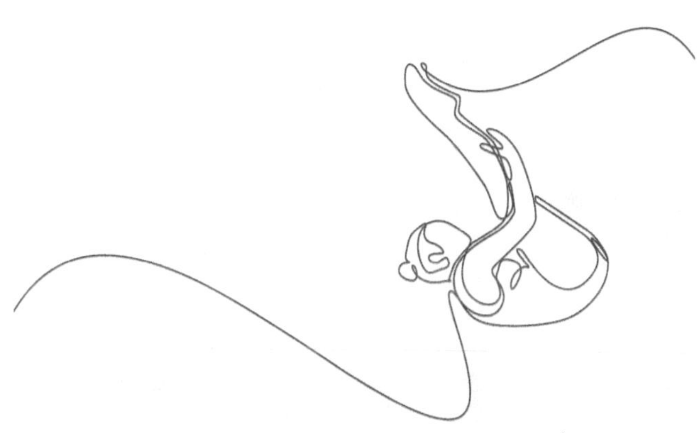

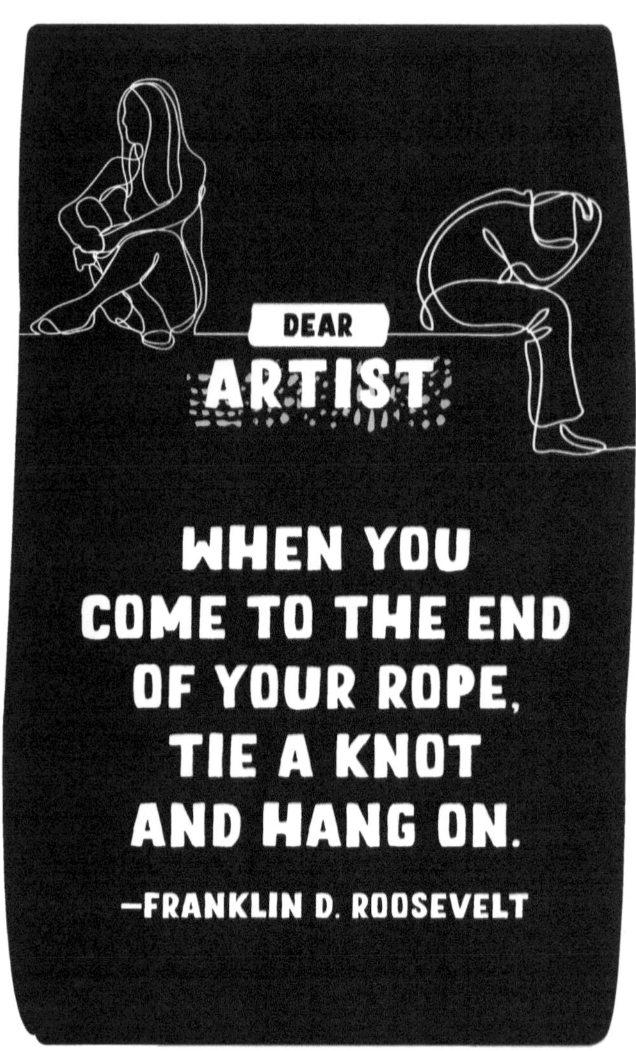
DEAR
ARTIST

WHEN YOU
COME TO THE END
OF YOUR ROPE,
TIE A KNOT
AND HANG ON.
—FRANKLIN D. ROOSEVELT

DEAR ARTIST,

The goal is to reveal. It's not about trying to put on a fake front or "pretend" somehow. While there is some element of "acting" going on in every performance, what you are shooting for is a revealing of your honest humanity, however that might show itself.

Because the audience doesn't come to see you. They come to see themselves.

And the way you show them that is by being authentic to *your*self.

Reveal the truth you connect to, and they will relate to the vulnerable human element you dare to be honest enough to show them.

Whether your platform is a canvas, recording studio, notebook, or traditional stage, your authentic vulnerability is what will speak to the masses.

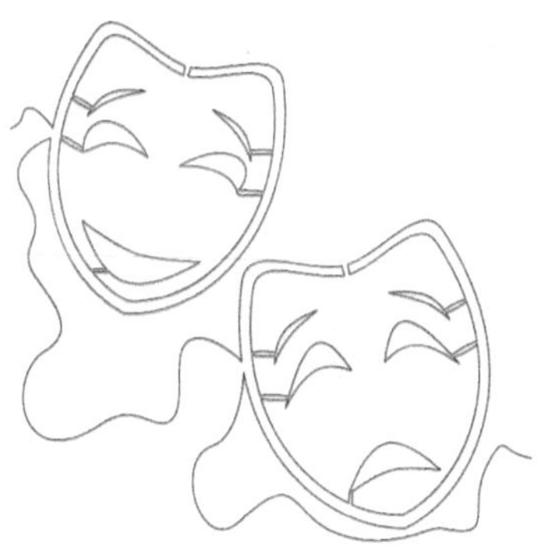

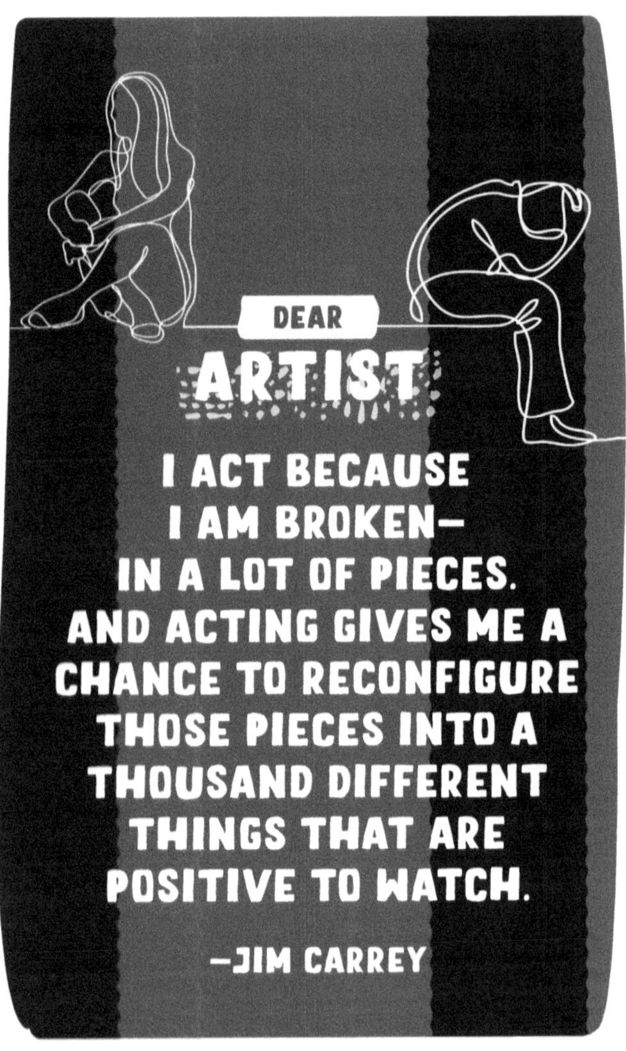

DEAR
ARTIST
I ACT BECAUSE
I AM BROKEN—
IN A LOT OF PIECES.
AND ACTING GIVES ME A
CHANCE TO RECONFIGURE
THOSE PIECES INTO A
THOUSAND DIFFERENT
THINGS THAT ARE
POSITIVE TO WATCH.
—JIM CARREY

DEAR ARTIST,

Redirection doesn't mean failure.

Sometimes things happen that are entirely out of your control.

Just when you feel like you're getting into a good groove, something happens to set you back ten steps. Your car breaks down, you have to move back home, your performance dates get canceled, your teacher abruptly quits...

What might you be being led to?

Maybe instead of dancing, you're supposed to write a book for a while. Or for a season, your paintbrush should be exchanged for sculptor's clay. Have you always wanted to try your hand at songwriting? Or rather than classical composing, maybe the comedy club has been calling your name.

Life knows when it's just the right moment to balance out your creative scales. And that, in turn will strengthen your entire artistic self.

Use the difficulty, and flow with the redirection.

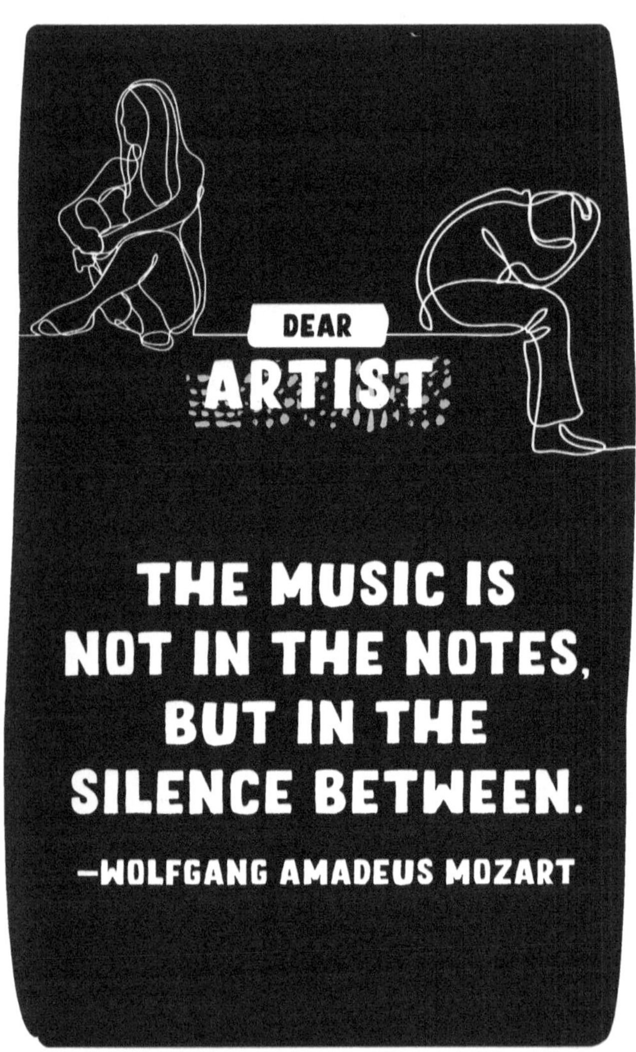
DEAR
ARTIST
THE MUSIC IS
NOT IN THE NOTES,
BUT IN THE
SILENCE BETWEEN.
—WOLFGANG AMADEUS MOZART

DEAR ARTIST,

Your time is not being wasted. You are one of the lucky few who have found the key that unlocks your heart. A treasure that gives your soul life. Most people never find that, but you have.

Your talent and craft are a gift.

You already have it, and no one can take it away.

The only question is: What are you going to do with it?

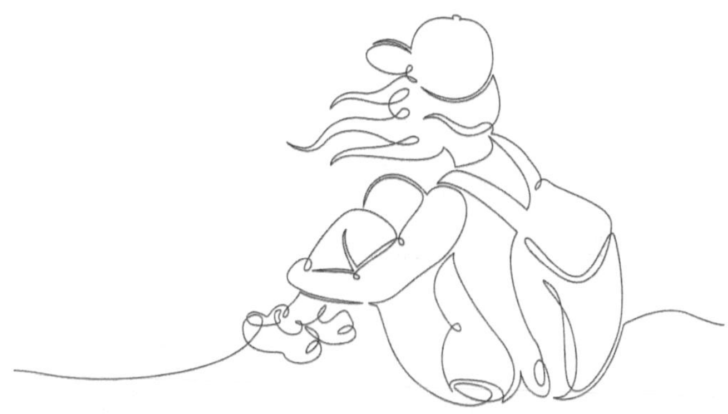

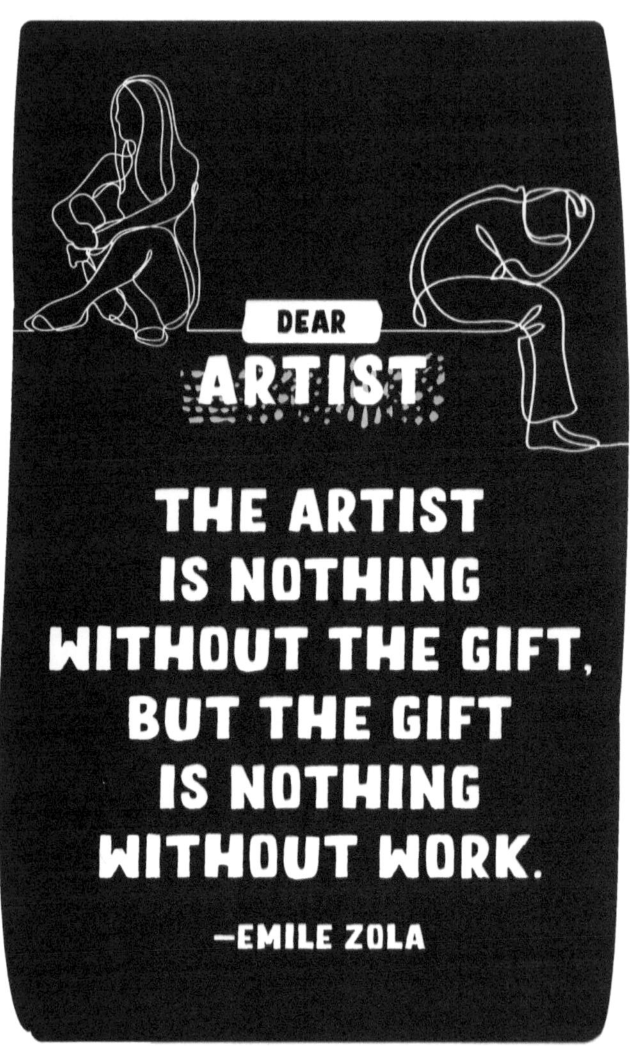
DEAR
ARTIST
THE ARTIST
IS NOTHING
WITHOUT THE GIFT,
BUT THE GIFT
IS NOTHING
WITHOUT WORK.
—EMILE ZOLA

DEAR ARTIST,

Let down the guard of your heart. You're safe. In this space, it's okay.

You've been going on fumes for so long, and you know that's not going to work any longer. Sometimes, because we know we need to heal (and we think we can't produce any more good work until we do) we panic. We become frantic and start looking around in a frenzy, trying to find the quickest and most efficient way to heal as soon as possible so we can get on with things already.

But that's not how healing works.

Healing takes faith. Trust in the process. That when you quiet your anxious heart, the healing will take over and lead you by the hand into it's restoring oasis. The process cannot happen while you are trying to make it happen.

Surrender.

Let down your guard. You need only be still.

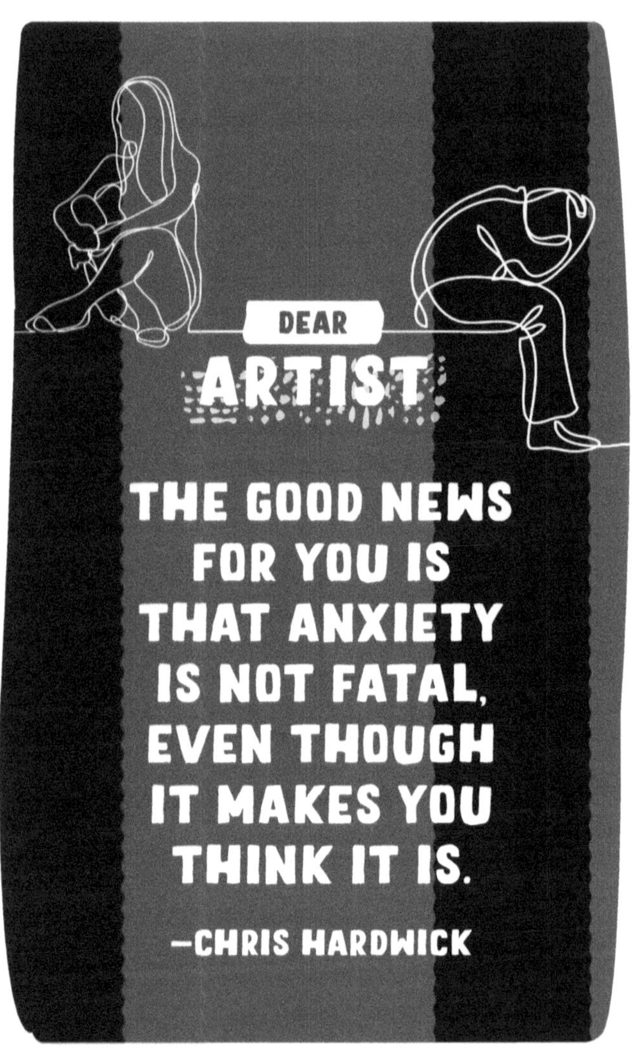
DEAR
ARTIST
THE GOOD NEWS
FOR YOU IS
THAT ANXIETY
IS NOT FATAL,
EVEN THOUGH
IT MAKES YOU
THINK IT IS.
—CHRIS HARDWICK

DEAR ARTIST,

If something is being laid on your heart to create or do, then of course, you owe it to yourself to make it happen.

But not only that. You owe it to the world.

Because if that thing keeps playing at your heart, that means someone somewhere needs to hear it's message.

You owe it to the teenager who will hear the bridge of your song and find strength to keep going. You owe it to the little girl who is going to grow up and become a dancer because she saw you perform. Even if you know you made mistakes, she doesn't. Your dancing is going to be the most beautiful thing she has ever seen.

You owe it to the middle-aged man who hasn't picked up his pencils to sketch in years. When he wanders into your gallery, your watercolors are going to be the final nudge he needs to pry open that dusty box filled with supplies, hopes, and dreams.

Yes, your art is 100% about you, but that's not all there is to it. Don't cheat the world of your greatness by refusing to carry on.

These people are real and they are out there. And whether they know it or not, they depend on you to be true to yourself.

As does your own soul.

So get up and let's get to work. You are needed for the bigger picture.

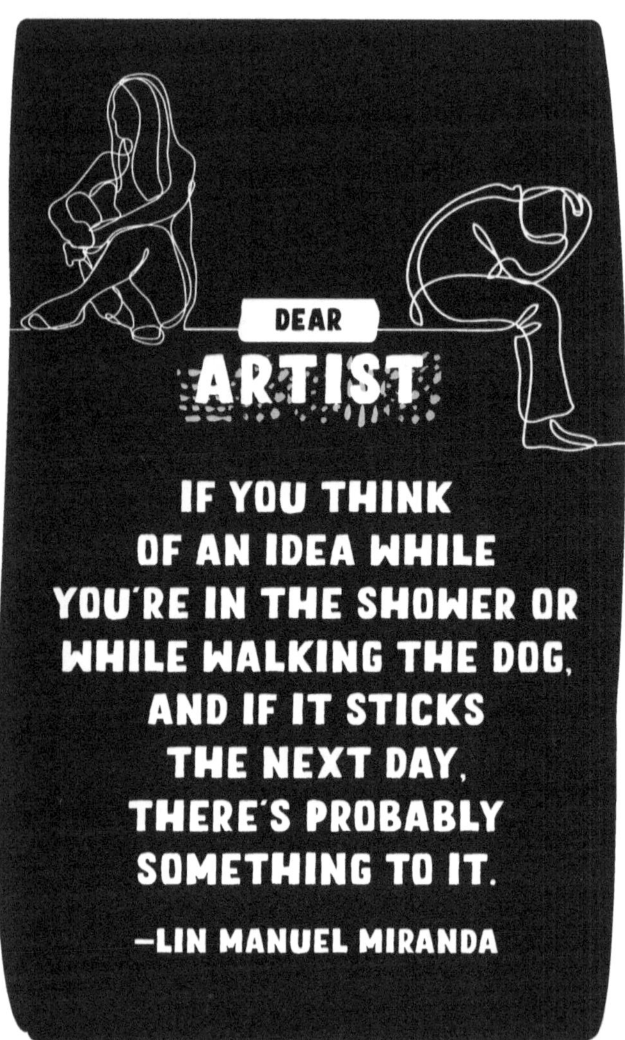
DEAR
ARTIST
IF YOU THINK
OF AN IDEA WHILE
YOU'RE IN THE SHOWER OR
WHILE WALKING THE DOG,
AND IF IT STICKS
THE NEXT DAY,
THERE'S PROBABLY
SOMETHING TO IT.
—LIN MANUEL MIRANDA

DEAR ARTIST,

If you don't know what step to take next, that's fine. Just step.

A rhythm sets in. You'll find your way. Bravery is not the absence of fear and doubt, it's feeling those things and walking anyway.

It's taking a step, even as your legs shake.

Just because it's hard doesn't mean you're on the wrong path.

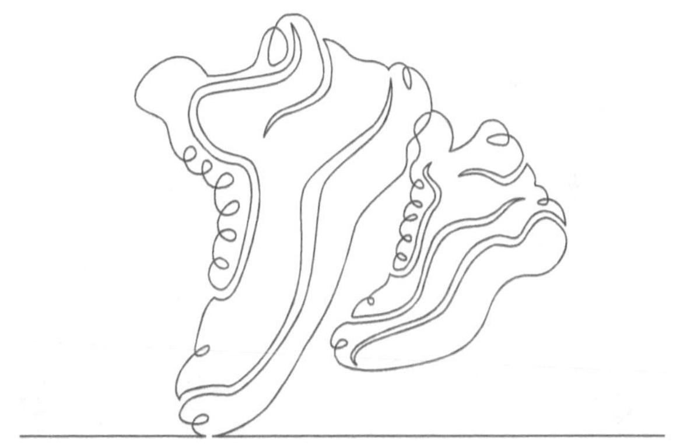

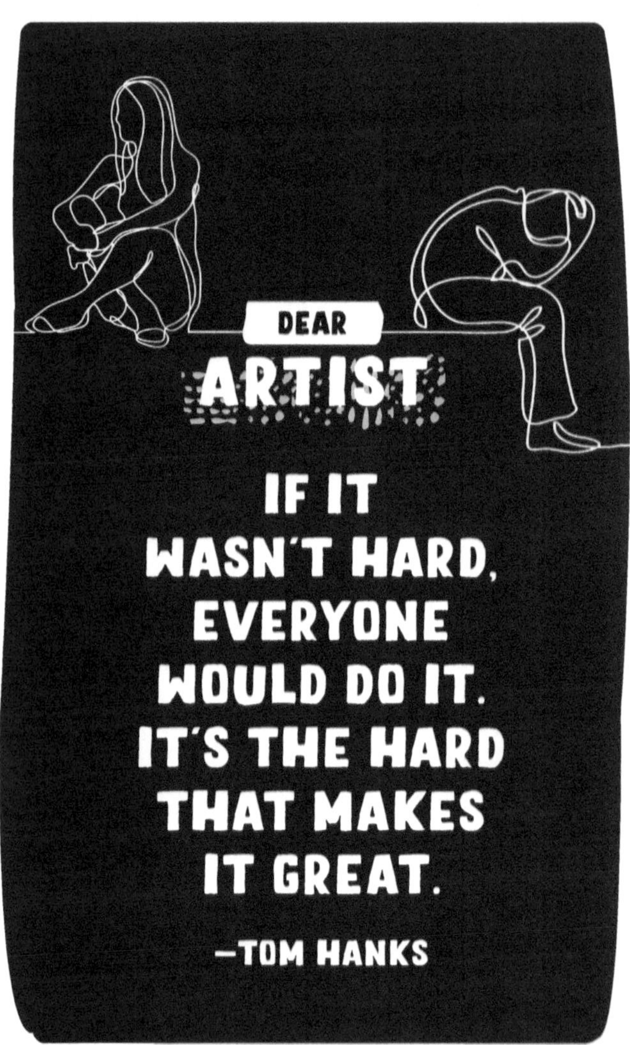

DEAR
ARTIST
IF IT WASN'T HARD, EVERYONE WOULD DO IT. IT'S THE HARD THAT MAKES IT GREAT.
—TOM HANKS

DEAR ARTIST,

I know how stuck you feel. Between a rock and a hard place. Sometimes it's better for our soul and our art if we step away for awhile and take stock of ourselves. Take a rest. You've been working so hard and you've made so much progress.

What do you have that's just for you? Something not tied to the bills or this way of life you've chosen? Rest and another mode of artistic expression is often the key to reopening the flow of inspiration, guidance, and motivation.

Go easy on yourself. You're doing incredible.

And you deserve every bit of kindness that you so readily afford to everyone else.

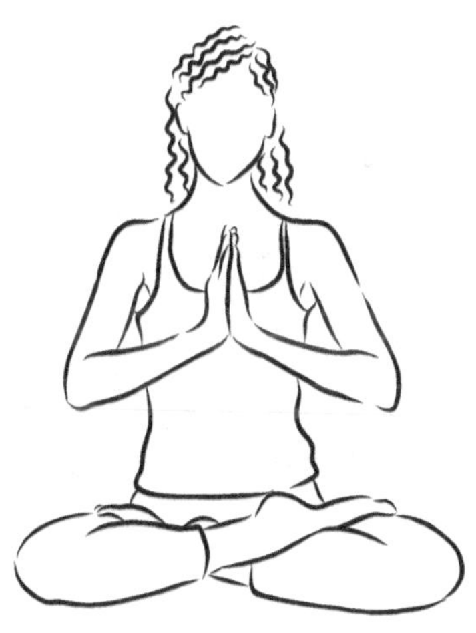

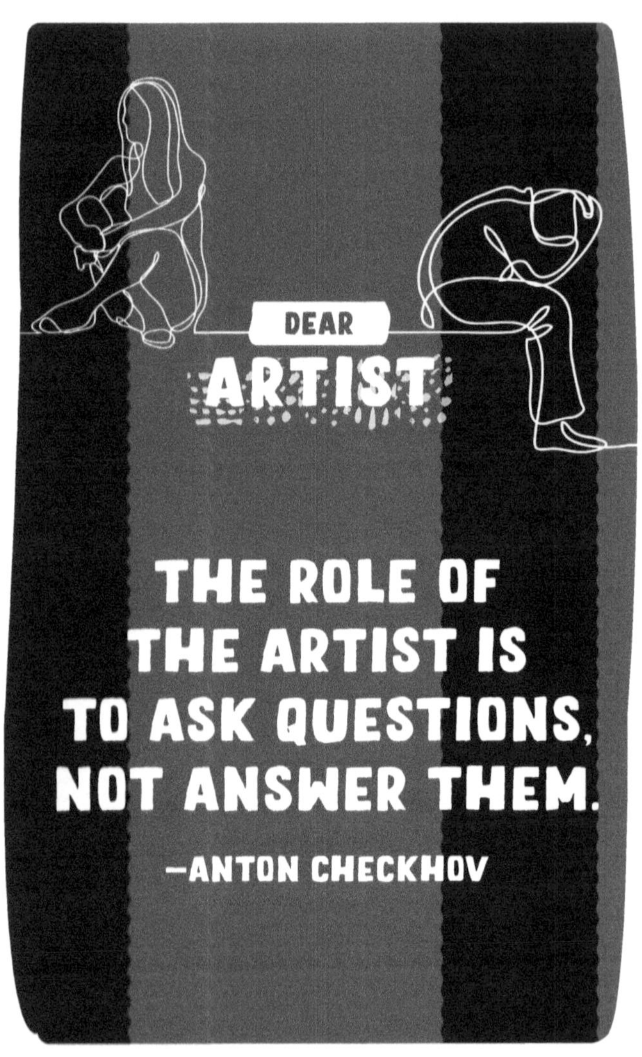

DEAR
ARTIST

THE ROLE OF
THE ARTIST IS
TO ASK QUESTIONS,
NOT ANSWER THEM.
—ANTON CHECKHOV

DEAR ARTIST,

Stop for a minute.

Close your eyes.

Refocus.

You are not falling short.

You are not failing.

Mountains are climbed by every little step.

Battles are won by every act of bravery.

You are winning.

You are conquering.

You beautiful warrior, you.

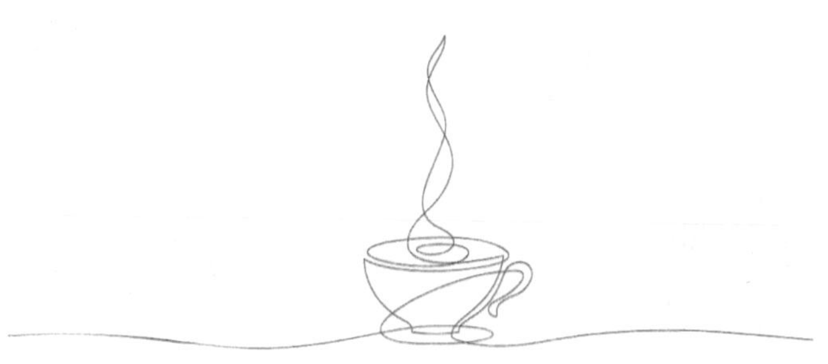

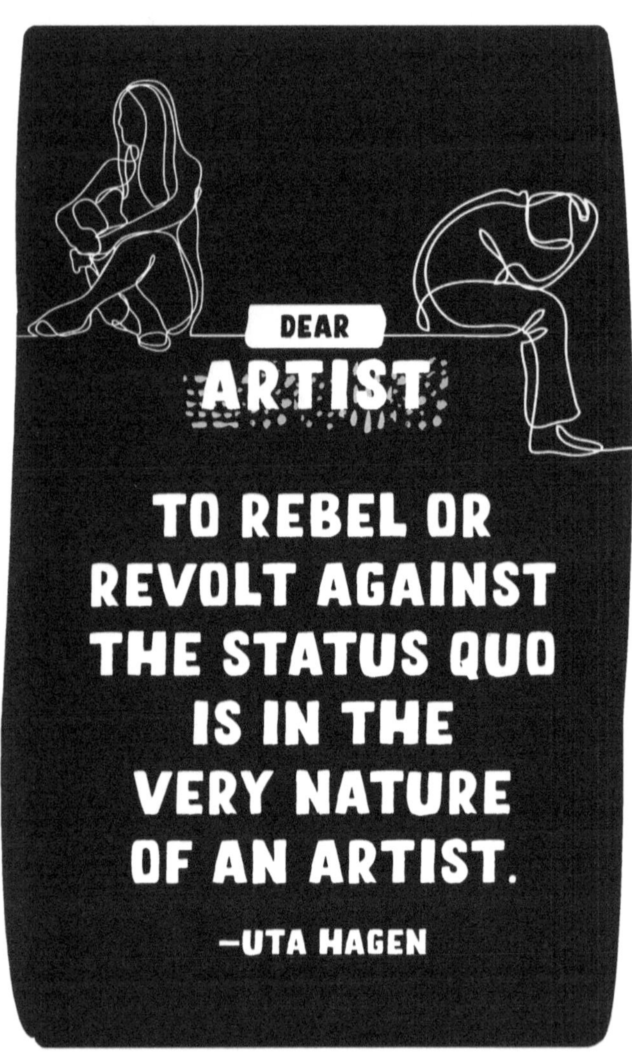

DEAR
ARTIST

TO REBEL OR
REVOLT AGAINST
THE STATUS QUO
IS IN THE
VERY NATURE
OF AN ARTIST.

-UTA HAGEN

DEAR ARTIST,

Don't discount your own feelings simply because other people have it worse. Regardless of whether or not that's true, it doesn't invalidate what you are thinking and feeling. Just because someone else may be going through a different kind of pain doesn't mean that yours doesn't hurt. Or that a loss doesn't knock the wind out of you.

Sometimes those creative losses hit harder than we expect and it shocks us. We try to downplay the pain, telling ourselves it's silly or stupid to feel this way.

It's not silly. It's not stupid. It's healing and necessary.

This thing you lost meant something to you. It carried weight and value. And if the rug has all of a sudden been pulled out from under you, it's going to hurt when your head hits the floor.

Feel the pain. Mourn the loss. For its own sake, because it was a worthwhile endeavor, and also so that you might heal and be able to move on without creative scar tissue forming.

Don't deny the things you feel.

Your hurt is just as valid as anyone else's.

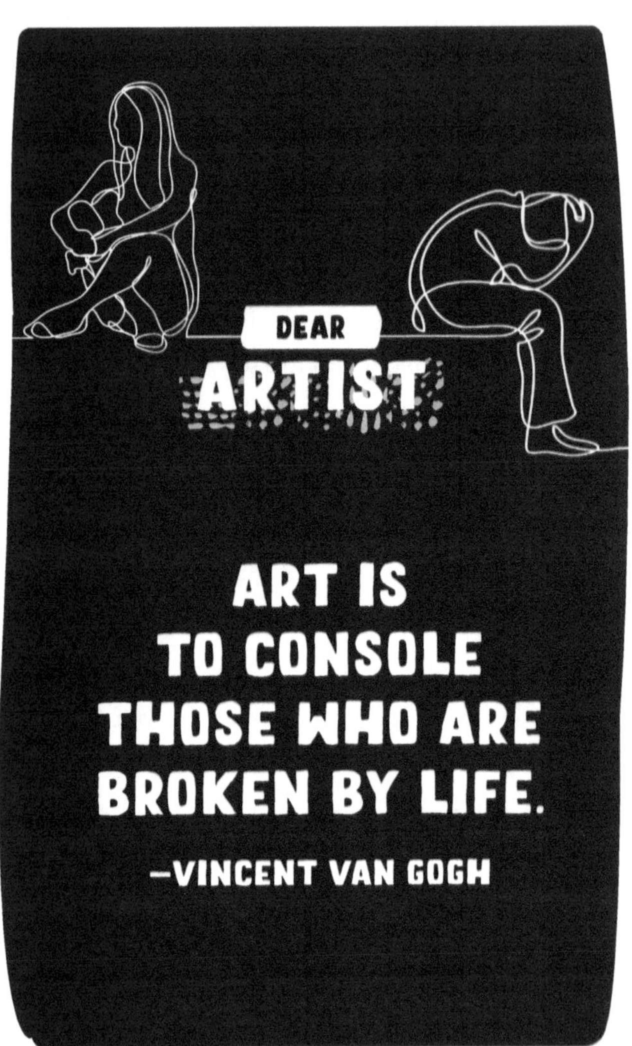
DEAR
ARTIST

ART IS
TO CONSOLE
THOSE WHO ARE
BROKEN BY LIFE.
—VINCENT VAN GOGH

DEAR ARTIST,

The lives that artists lead make up a sort of genealogy. Each of your heroes and every person that you've been influenced by form a sort of spiritual ancestry that you have the awesome privilege of carrying on

All of their brilliance, all of their art, all of their laboring work has come down to this. Their genius meets with yours.

When we first start out, we copy, we imitate, we trace. As we should. That is the nature of the work. But as we grow and develop our technique, what was once an imitation becomes a knit together tapestry.

We have the privilege of being next in line in an ancestry made up, not only of our personal heroes, but of some of the world's greatest minds, creatives and free-thinkers. Feel the gravity of such an honor, and take it seriously.

Whose work do you enjoy? What about them inspires you? Trace the lines that they have masterfully perfected. Study the way they move, speak, play, and live. Then figure out who inspired them. Sooner than you think, you will no longer be emulating. You will be creating something new, fully your own, with hints and threads of your greatest heroes' work woven into yours.

Copy. Pretend. Take the first few wobbly steps. And in time, you will find yourself integrating into the family of that which you love so dearly.

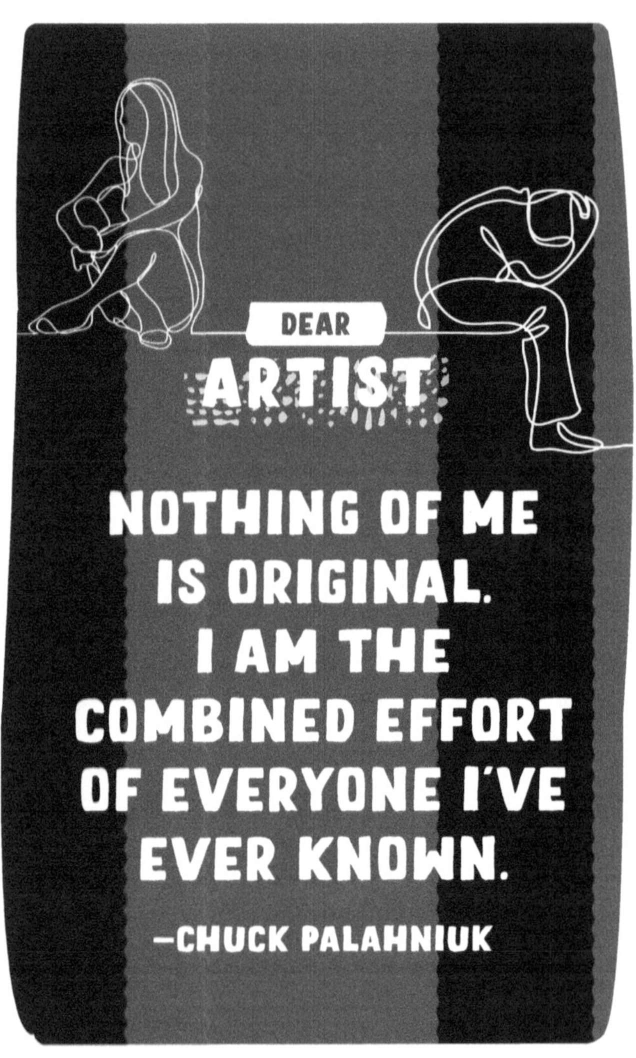
DEAR
ARTIST

NOTHING OF ME
IS ORIGINAL.
I AM THE
COMBINED EFFORT
OF EVERYONE I'VE
EVER KNOWN.

-CHUCK PALAHNIUK

DEAR ARTIST,

Stop listening to everyone around you. They don't have your intel, they don't have your insight, and they don't have your driving force of a soul. Listening to others who have no understanding of your artist's psyche will only make you anxious, fearful, and question your well thought out decisions. Decisions that you have meticulously gone over time and time again. For your sanity and wellbeing, stop listening to others opinions.

Opinions are just that—opinions. Not facts. Tune them out.

You have to.

It is crucial for your spirit's survival.

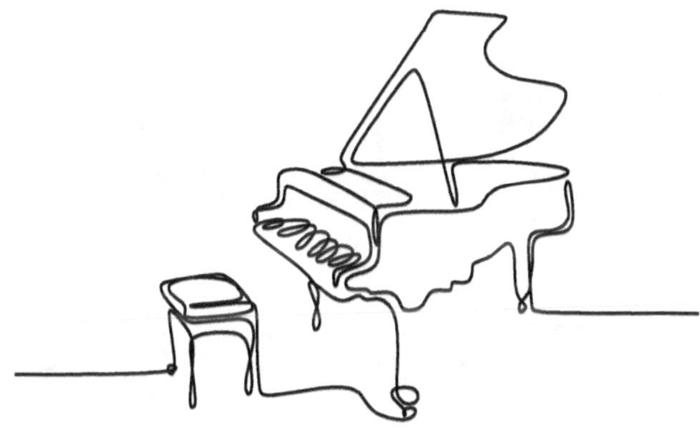

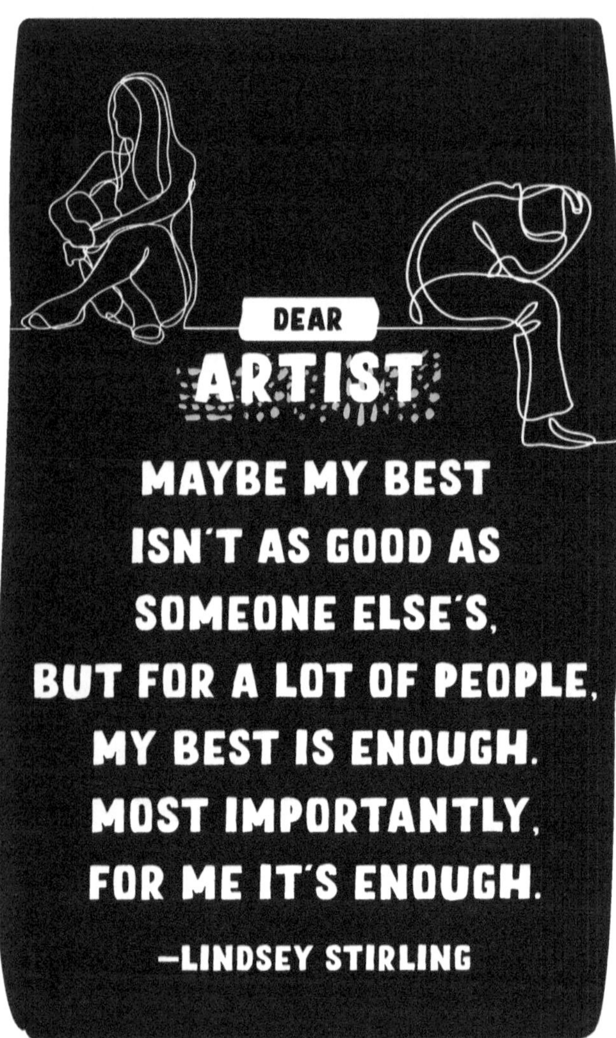
DEAR
ARTIST
MAYBE MY BEST
ISN'T AS GOOD AS
SOMEONE ELSE'S,
BUT FOR A LOT OF PEOPLE,
MY BEST IS ENOUGH.
MOST IMPORTANTLY,
FOR ME IT'S ENOUGH.
—LINDSEY STIRLING

DEAR ARTIST,

Failure is like a staircase. And it's only direction is up.

Each step on that staircase of failure takes you closer and closer to the destination of success.

You fail up.

And every time you fall flat on your face, take a moment to be grateful. Because every step you climb puts you one step closer to the top.

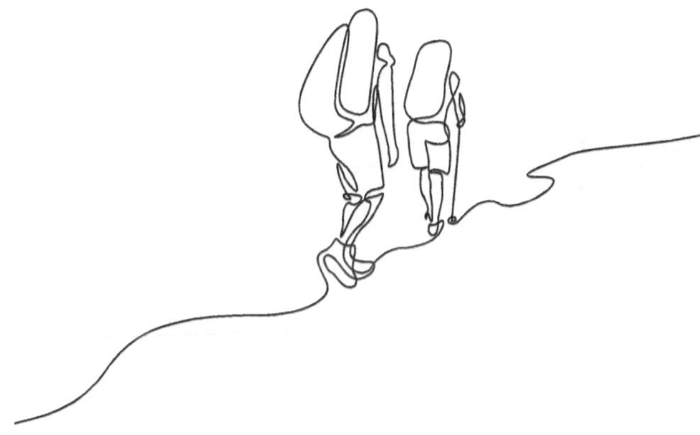

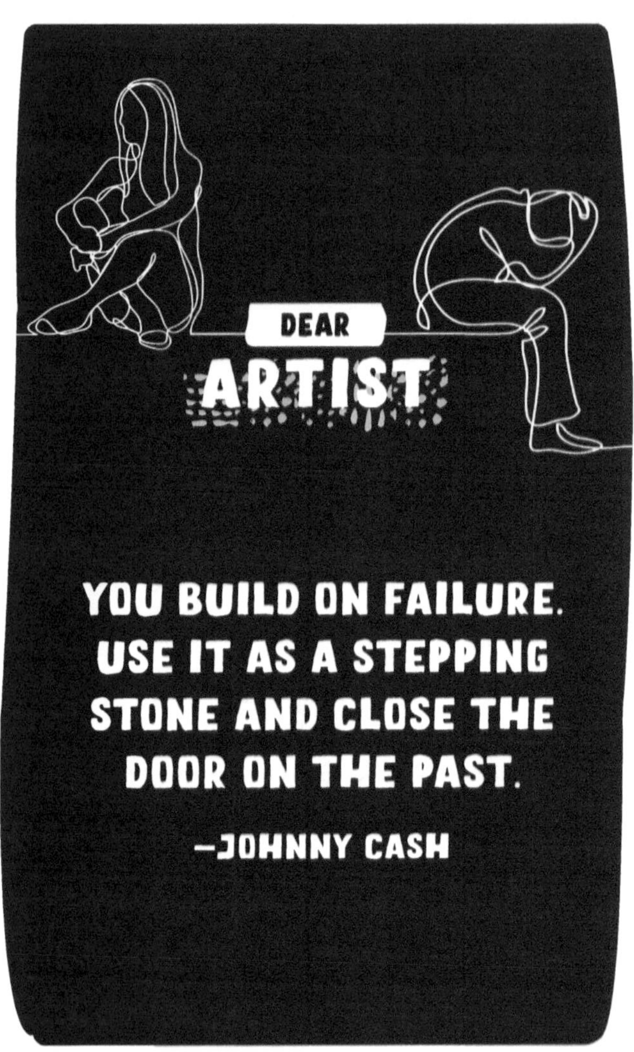
DEAR
ARTIST

YOU BUILD ON FAILURE.
USE IT AS A STEPPING
STONE AND CLOSE THE
DOOR ON THE PAST.

—JOHNNY CASH

DEAR ARTIST,

Stop going so hard for the moment. You think that you are doing yourself and your career a favor, but you're not. The pace and intensity are killing you.

You cannot help anyone else if you are too weak, tired, and broken to stand. Let alone create.

Slow down.

Heal.

Your number one priority right now is to take your time and heal.

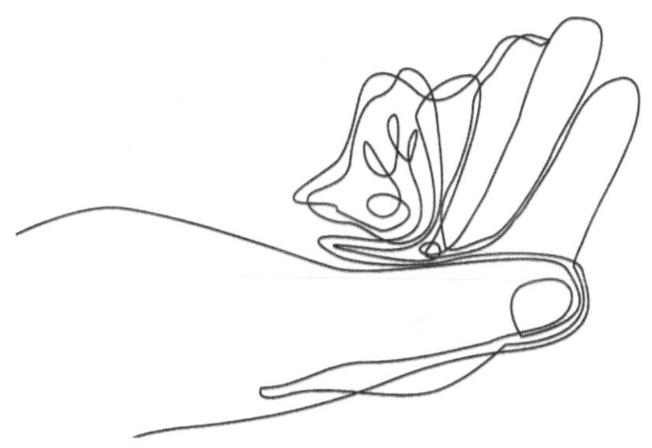

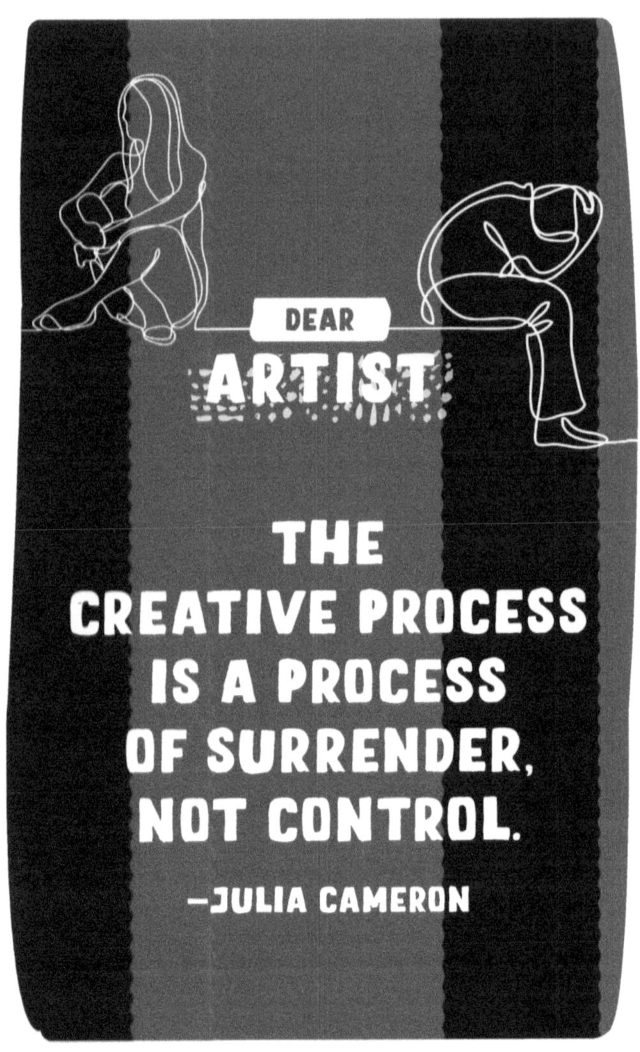

DEAR
ARTIST
THE
CREATIVE PROCESS
IS A PROCESS
OF SURRENDER,
NOT CONTROL.
—JULIA CAMERON

DEAR ARTIST,

Picasso once said, "Good artists borrow. Great artists steal." And he couldn't have been more correct.

Artists steal. That's just the simple fact of it.

If you see a piece of art that perks you up and makes you go, "That's very clever, I like that." Take it! Learn from it! Use it! It doesn't matter if it's from a painting, manuscript, or performance. Study how the artist did it, then take it and incorporate it into your own work. There is a very high chance that the person you're watching stole it from someone else, who in turn stole it from someone else.

You will steal from other artists. Just make sure that when you do, you only steal from the best.

Because if you steal from the best, you have a very good chance of joining their ranks.

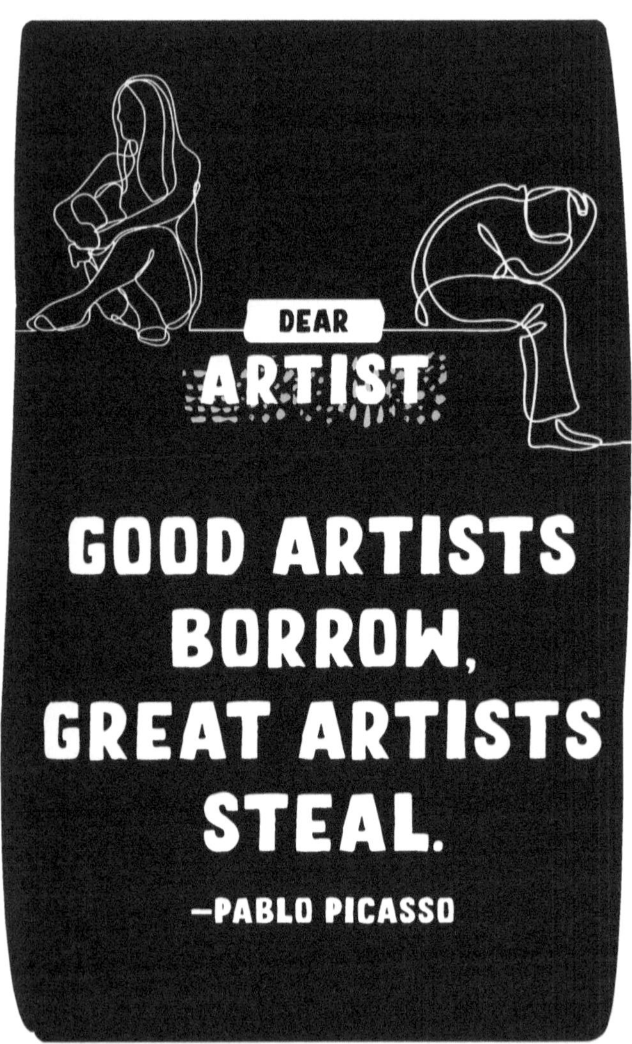

DEAR
ARTIST

GOOD ARTISTS
BORROW,
GREAT ARTISTS
STEAL.
—PABLO PICASSO

DEAR ARTIST,

Your creativity is not something to be afraid of or intimidated by.

Like a wild stallion that is yours to break, so is the tidal wave of emotion that rages within you.

Let its power invigorate you. The beast is yours to harness.

You have the ability. If only you will pick up the reins.

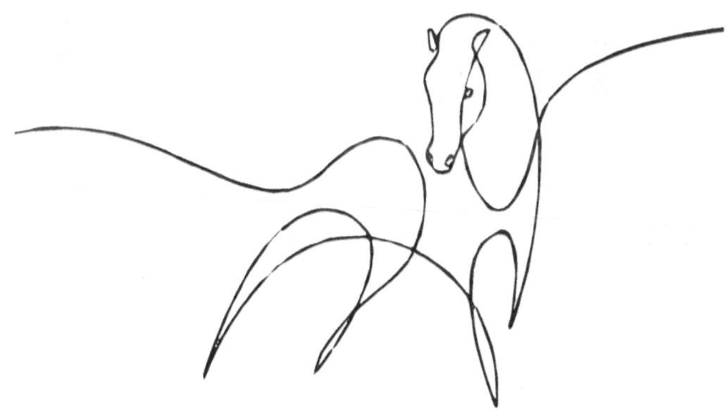

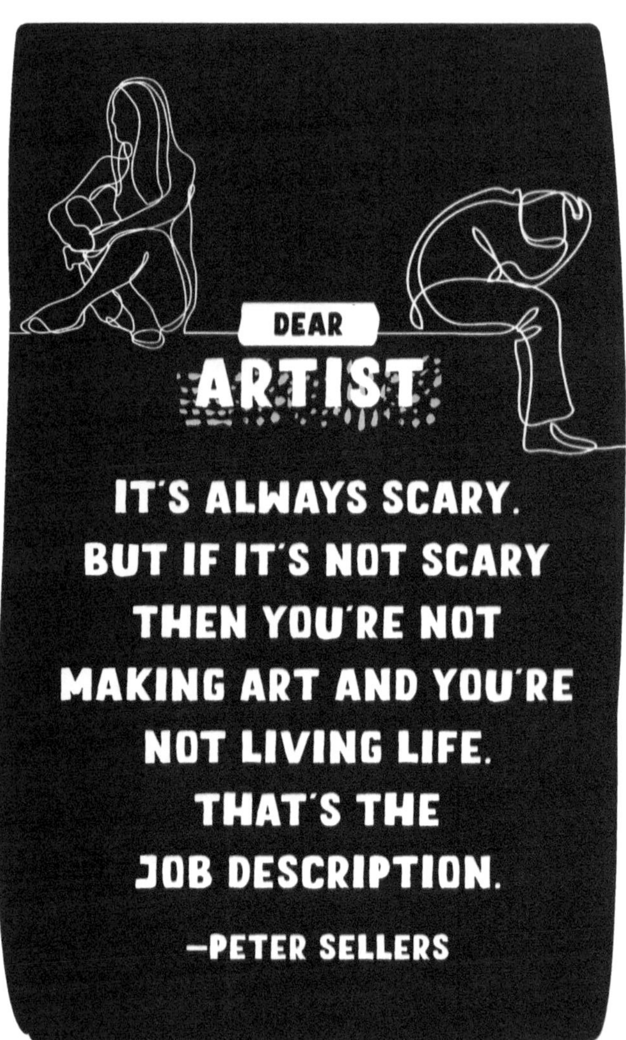

DEAR
ARTIST

IT'S ALWAYS SCARY.
BUT IF IT'S NOT SCARY
THEN YOU'RE NOT
MAKING ART AND YOU'RE
NOT LIVING LIFE.
THAT'S THE
JOB DESCRIPTION.

—PETER SELLERS

DEAR ARTIST,

You may think that when you're creating, the more general you are, the more people you'll reach. I have actually found the opposite to be true.

The more specific you are to your own experience, the wider an audience you will impact and the more people will see themselves in your story.

Your audience connects to that human part of you that you are sharing. And even if they have not found themselves in the exact same situation as you, they will subconsciously take and apply it to their own similar circumstances.

Lives are touched and people are changed through specific honesty.

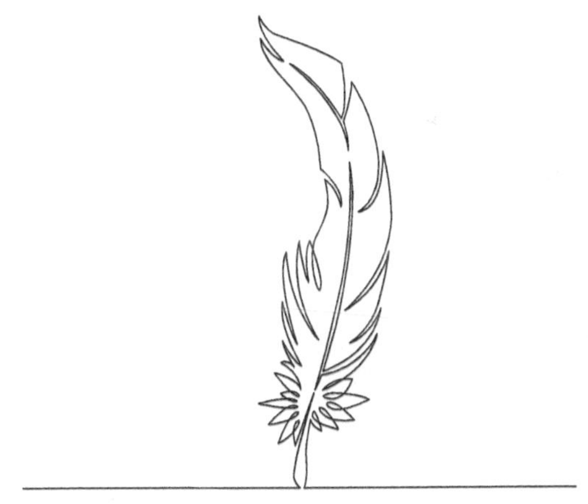

DEAR ARTIST,

Our default setting is one of insecurity. We feel like frauds because we are constantly in our heads, wondering if the thing we've made actually has any value, and feeling like we don't fit in among the *real* artists.

I know. I'm right there with you.

Imposter syndrome tends to run high in artists because creatives are more inclined to have a high emotional intelligence. Since this is the case, we tend to see others as just as talented and deserving as we are, and because of that we often downplay our own ideas and accomplishments, thinking that everyone else has ideas that are just as good or better than ours. This leads us to dismiss our thoughts and ideas entirely. Or if we do get up the courage to forge ahead and act on those ideas, we often then hide the finished results, or talk them down when other people finally see them, thinking that we aren't worthy of praise.

I believe that the very fact that you are questioning your work proves that it is very much worthwhile. You are not just one of those people bragging about their achievements out of arrogance and a lack of self-awareness.

And those people that you feel so intimidated by? Most of them feel just the same way. Not knowing whether their ideas and work have the value they so hope and pray they do.

You aren't fooling anybody because there is nothing to be fooled by. Your talent is real.

Your ideas, accomplishments, and hard work are all real.

The thing you're working on at this very moment has real, tangible value.

And no, I'm not just saying that.

Every true artist that I've ever known has had imposter syndrome to some degree or another.

And I've come to see it almost as a friend. Or at least a sign.

If it's there, I'm on the right track. And you are too.

The creative space is not an exclusive club.

You are worthy to be at the table, just as much as anyone else.

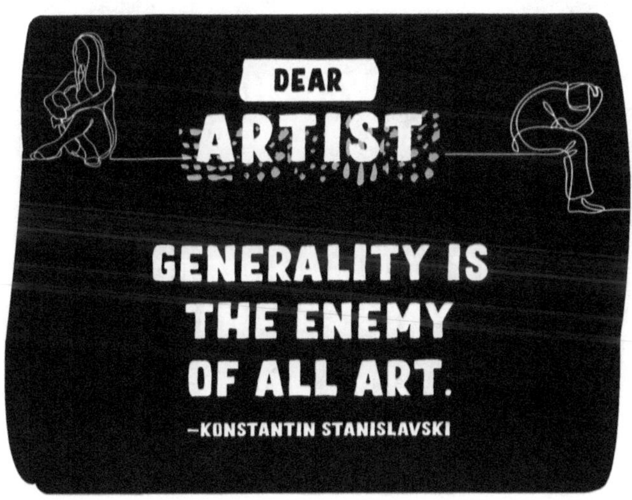

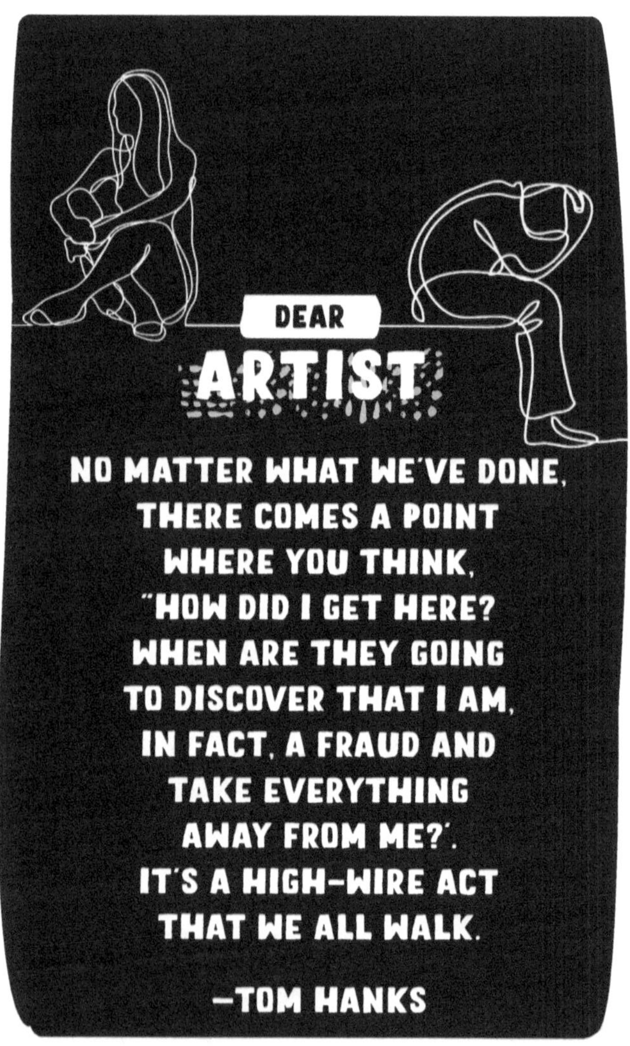

DEAR
ARTIST

NO MATTER WHAT WE'VE DONE,
THERE COMES A POINT
WHERE YOU THINK,
"HOW DID I GET HERE?
WHEN ARE THEY GOING
TO DISCOVER THAT I AM,
IN FACT, A FRAUD AND
TAKE EVERYTHING
AWAY FROM ME?".
IT'S A HIGH-WIRE ACT
THAT WE ALL WALK.

—TOM HANKS

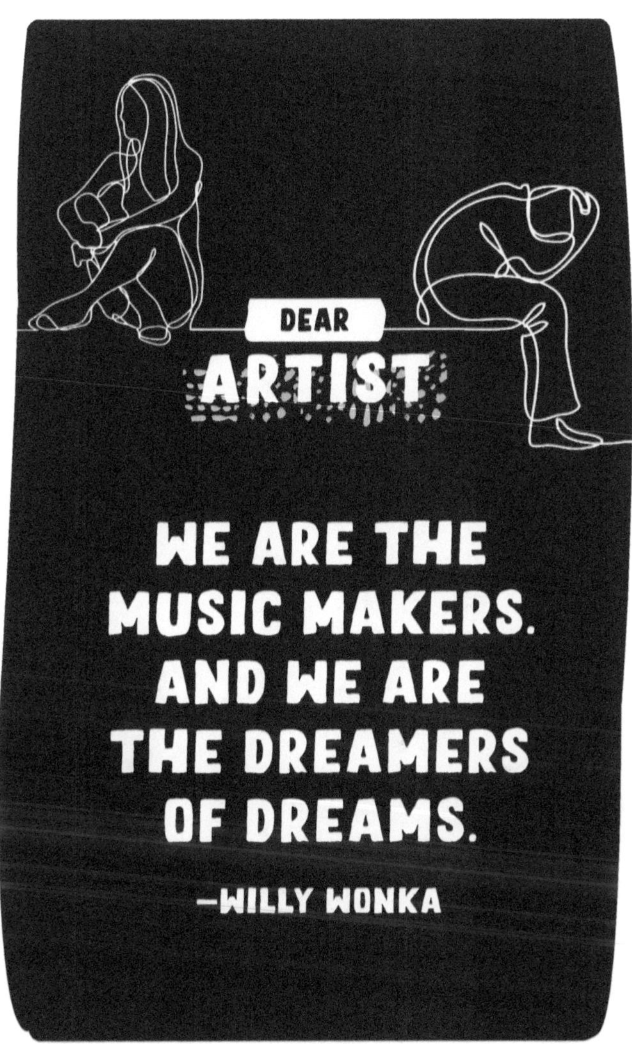
DEAR
ARTIST
WE ARE THE
MUSIC MAKERS.
AND WE ARE
THE DREAMERS
OF DREAMS.
—WILLY WONKA

DEAR ARTIST,

You are enough.

In this moment.

Just as you are.

You are enough.

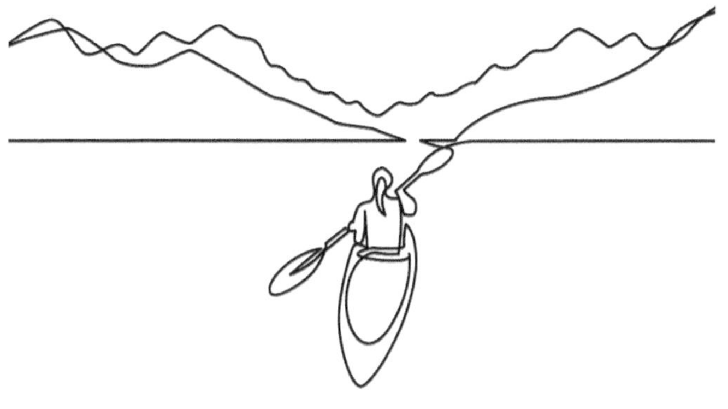